SKI TOWN Brunch

EXCEPTIONAL BRUNCHES *from* WORLD CLASS SKI RESORTS

JENNIE IVERSON

SKI TOWN GROUP Ltd.

Library of Congress: 2019905503

ISBN 13: 978-0-9857290-1-1

Manufactured in China by Pettit Network Inc.

For photography credits, see end section.
Book Design and typesetting by James Monroe Design, LLC.

For information about special purchases or custom editions, please contact:
info@skitownlife.com. Ski Town Group, Ltd. is the publishing firm for Ski Town Life.

Ski Town Life
2121 N. Frontage Road, W. #5
Vail, Colorado 81657

www.skitownlife.com

 @skitownlife

 @skitownlife

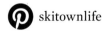 skitownlife

Ski Town Brunch is dedicated to my family of gentlemen: Ross, Hunter, Grant and Brooks. In my sons' growing prowess, breakfast time has turned into sleeping late and lingering over brunch time or even second breakfasts during the morning.

Our ski town living is a lifestyle—we can only embrace the complete extent of it fully energized and fueled. So gents, eat some breakfast, and then make your stamp on the world!

CONTENTS

CONTENTS
Listed by Ski Resort

Ski Town Brunch Background

The *Ski Town Brunch* cookbook celebrates the start of the day by featuring unique breakfast and brunch recipes from charming bed and breakfasts to luxury hotels. It blends passion for energizing your soul and fueling your body. This is a must-have keepsake for skiers, foodies and travelers. Like *Ski Town Soups* and *Ski Town Après Ski* (the first 2 cookbooks in the Ski Town Cookbook Collection), *Ski Town Brunch* is a beautiful, colorful rendition of over 60 North American world-class ski resorts, fun-loving restaurants and scrumptious brunch recipes. Enjoy this cookbook of savory and sweet starters that you can enjoy throughout the ski season, as well as during the rest of the year. From the various eclectic flavor profiles with regional flair to even the most classic breakfast dish; many of the inspired recipes originate from fresh and locally-sourced ingredients, which are close to the chefs' hearts and elevate the ski town cuisine.

Indulge in this cookbook for a taste and visual tour of how ski towns "do brunch." Because, brunch is always a good idea!

Winning Restaurants Determined

To determine the included restaurants, Ski Town Life conducted extensive online research, along with periodical ratings and guidance. The brunch scene was incredibly important when it came to choosing the featured restaurants. The unique and wide food offerings as well as the restaurants' and resorts culture and ambiance all factored into the selection process. Restaurant reviews and recommendations, both online and through travelers/guests, were taken into account. Based on the research results, the *Ski Town Brunch* cookbook highlights the most beloved breakfast and brunch restaurants in over 60 world-class North American ski towns. The restaurants range from charming bed and breakfasts to luxury resorts located in the same ski town as the ski resort, or relatively close to the associated ski resort.

Cookbook Usability

This cookbook is divided into 3 sections, which are grouped as savories, sweets, sides and sips (alas, alliteration always appeals). At the beginning of the cookbook, there are 2 Tables of Contents: 1—by food category and 2—by ski resort. This usability appeals to foodies and home cooks, as well as travelers and skiers.

Each recipe is rated with a "difficulty level" that should be familiar to winter enthusiasts. The green circle indicates a relatively easy recipe, or a recipe that can be tackled immediately. The green circle recipes ● should be approachable to all cooks. The blue square ■ is a bit more difficult, or intermediate level. This recipe should be within most home cooks' capabilities, but may take a little longer. The black diamond recipes ◆ are the most advanced recipes in the cookbook, and may challenge even the most adept home cook. Sample the black diamond recipes on a weekend, when you have ample time. Have fun with these ratings! It's not a scientific rating system; levels of difficulty were merely estimated by amount of time to complete the recipe, special techniques used, and number and availability of the ingredients.

Own the Collection

The Ski Town Cookbook Collection is comprised of over 400 recipes from unique venues across North American ski towns.

Ski Town Soups presents a perfectly balanced recipe for life: a ski town, a comfortable restaurant, and a yummy bowl of soup.

Ski Town Après Ski captures the essence of the après ski scene by pairing appetizing plates and handcrafted cocktails.

Ski Town Brunch highlights recipes from charming bed and breakfasts to luxury resorts, setting an energizing tone for the rest of the day.

Ski Town Journey Continued

Purchase the box set or individual titles through our retail partners or at **SkiTownLife.com**. Sign-up at **SkiTownLife.com** for custom recipes to add to your collection, newsletter and blog posts, and other interesting culinary tidbits.

SAVORIES

WALDORF ASTORIA PARK CITY
EGGS BENEDICT

WALDORF ASTORIA PARK CITY • PARK CITY, UTAH

Waldorf Astoria Park City, set in the Canyons Village, provides exclusive access to skiing and snowboarding within Park City Resort, the largest ski resort in the United States. Start the day with a fantastic range of luxury breakfast choices and experience elevated comfort food inspired by mountain regions around the world.

1 Tbsp. white distilled vinegar

8 large eggs

4 English muffins, split and toasted

8 slices smoked salmon

2 Tbsp. unsalted butter

Tomato Marmalade, see recipe

Hollandaise Sauce, see recipe

Chives, chopped

Kosher salt

Black pepper, coarsely ground

SERVES 4

SERVING SUGGESTION:
Sprinkle finished Eggs Benedict
with chives, sea salt and
black pepper.

MORE DIFFICULT

Fill medium pot with 3 inches water, add vinegar, season with salt and simmer. Stir water clockwise with a handle of a spoon and gently crack egg into center of pot. Repeat with remaining eggs, up to four at a time. Check eggs after 4 minutes: use a slotted spoon to lift egg out of water, the whites should be just set. Remove eggs and drain on a paper towel-lined plate.

Liberally butter and add Tomato Marmalade to toasted English muffin halves and top each with a slice of smoked salmon and a poached egg. Spoon Hollandaise Sauce over the eggs.

TOMATO MARMALADE

2 lbs. ripe tomatoes

2 ¼ cups sugar

Black pepper

Kosher salt

2 ¼ tsp. lemon juice

Boil water in large saucepan. Remove the stem of each tomato and slice a shallow X in the bottom. Plunge tomatoes into boiling water until skins loosen, about 30 seconds. Remove from water and cool, then remove skins. Halve tomatoes and gently squeeze out seeds and any excess liquid. Return tomatoes to empty saucepan and stir in sugar, pepper, and salt. Cook over medium heat, stirring frequently until liquid has reduced. Remove from heat and stir in lemon juice. Ladle marmalade into clean jars, cover tightly, cool and refrigerate.

HOLLANDAISE SAUCE

¾ cup unsalted butter

3 large egg yolks

2 ¼ tsp. fresh lemon juice, plus more to taste

Cayenne pepper

Kosher salt

Simmer 1-inch water in saucepan. In a small pot, melt butter over medium heat until foamy, 3 - 4 minutes. In a stainless steel bowl, whisk egg yolks and 1 Tbsp. cold water until light and foamy. Continue whisking while adding a couple of drops of lemon juice. Set the bowl directly atop the saucepan of simmering water. The water should not come in contact with the bottom of the bowl. Whisk eggs for 1 - 2 minutes, until slightly thickened. Remove bowl from heat and add warm, melted butter slowly, while whisking constantly. Add remaining lemon juice and season with salt and cayenne. The finished sauce will have a smooth, firm consistency. If it's too thick, you can adjust the consistency by whisking in a few drops of warm water.

EGG WHITE FRITTATA

GRAND HYATT VAIL • CHEF JAY SPICKELMIER • VAIL, COLORADO

Chef Jay Spickelmier proudly states that his "passion for cooking is found in the adventurous Rocky Mountain lifestyle and all that Vail and the surrounding area has to offer. Finding new inspiration to define Rocky Mountain Cuisine only requires a quick glance at the natural beauty that surrounds us." Therefore, one will see the mountain inspiration in every aspect of Grand Hyatt Vail's cuisine. Food and drink celebrate the culinary heritage of the Colorado Rockies. This inventive blend of cultures echoes Vail's own heritage at Grand Hyatt Vail.

¼ cup spinach, blanched

¼ cup sun-dried tomatoes, julienned

4 egg whites

2 oz. goat cheese, crumbled

Salt and pepper

SERVES 1

Warm spinach and tomatoes in omelette pan, add whisked egg whites, cook to set bottom. Sprinkle goat cheese on top and place under the broiler to set top. Season to taste with salt and pepper.

SERVING SUGGESTION:
Serve with country potatoes or hash browns.

MAPLE PICKLED DEVILED EGGS

LYNN BRITT CABIN • CHEF JIM BUTCHART • ASPEN, COLORADO

Lynn Britt Cabin combines elegance, Western ambiance and gourmet cuisine with the beauty and seclusion of an on-mountain restaurant. This quaint and romantic cabin is a spectacular setting for brunch, lunch or après ski. Inside the rustic yet elegant dining room or outside on the patio you will find a menu of gourmet Colorado cuisine at its finest.

12 eggs, hard boiled and peeled

1 ¼ cups water

1 cup apple cider vinegar

½ cup maple syrup

¼ cup brown sugar

1 cup sour cream

Salt

Black pepper

Maple Glazed Bacon, see recipe

Chives or green onions, for garnish

MAKES 24 DEVILED EGGS

 MORE DIFFICULT Bring water, vinegar, maple syrup, brown sugar, and pinch of salt to a boil. Pour hot liquid over peeled, hard boiled eggs, making sure they are completely covered. Cover and refrigerate overnight. Remove eggs from pickling liquid. With a sharp knife, slice each egg in half lengthwise. Wipe knife clean after each slice to keep egg whites clean. With a small spoon, scoop egg yolks into a bowl, reserve. Combine egg yolks, sour cream, and pinch of salt and pepper in food processor. Blend until smooth and creamy. With a rubber spatula, scoop filling into a piping bag. Pipe approximately 1 Tbsp. egg filling into cavity of each egg white. Top each deviled egg with a cube of Maple Glazed Bacon.

MAPLE GLAZED BACON

1 lb. slab bacon

1 cup apple cider vinegar

¼ cup maple syrup

¼ cup brown sugar

½ tsp. cinnamon

Cut bacon into 24 equal cubes. Cook in a medium sauté pan, over low to medium heat for 15 - 20 minutes, stirring often, until crispy. Strain bacon and return to pan over low-medium heat. Add vinegar, maple syrup, brown sugar, and cinnamon. Stir often and cook until liquid is reduced by half and bacon is well glazed.

SERVING SUGGESTION:
Top each deviled egg with chopped chives or green onions.

ONE PAN BRITISH FRY-UP
with Montana Baked Beans & Huckleberry Jam

THE WILD TABLE • CHEF SHEENA ERNST • RED LODGE, MONTANA

After attending culinary school in London and staying several more years to live and work, Chef Ernst became very accustomed to this traditional English breakfast. Now, many items on The Wild Table menu represent her time spent in England. Traditionally this dish was a working-class staple to sustain long days of labor; and now, hearty enough for those long days on the ski slopes.

4 sausage links, your preference

8 slices bacon, cooked

2 cups Montana Baked Beans, see recipe

1 large tomato, quartered

3 Tbsp. olive oil

Salt and pepper

8 eggs

1 Tbsp. thyme, finely chopped

4 small cast-iron pans

Sourdough bread

Huckleberry jam

SERVES 4

 Preheat oven to 450 degrees. Place tomatoes in a glass pie pan and drizzle with olive oil, salt and pepper. Roast for 20 minutes. In 1 of 4 small cast-iron pans, layer 1 sausage link, 2 bacon strips, ½ cup baked beans, 1 cooked tomato quarter and 2 eggs. Sprinkle with salt, pepper and ¼ tsp. thyme. Repeat with remaining ingredients and pans. Bake 15 minutes or until egg whites are set.

MONTANA BAKED BEANS

3 Tbsp. vegetable oil

2 garlic cloves, minced

4 slices bacon, diced

2 onions, diced

1 Tbsp. onion powder

1 tsp. paprika

1 tsp. chili powder

4 cups soaked, rinsed and cooked pinto beans; reserving cooking liquid or 4 cans pinto beans; do not drain

2 Tbsp. brown sugar

2 Tbsp. Worcestershire sauce

½ cup ketchup

2 Tbsp. apple cider vinegar

2 Tbsp. molasses

Preheat the oven to 250 degrees. Heat oil in a large oven-proof pot over medium heat. Add bacon, onion, garlic and seasonings. Cook until onions are soft, 5 minutes. Add beans and 2 cups of cooking liquid (or the cans of beans with their liquid), brown sugar, ketchup, vinegar, Worcestershire and molasses. Simmer for 10 minutes. Cover and place in oven for 2 hours. Remove cover and cook for another 30 minutes, or until thick and bubbly.

SERVING SUGGESTION:
Serve with toasted sourdough spread with huckleberry jam.

THREE CHEESE QUICHE

THE CHINA CLIPPER INN • OURAY, COLORADO

Charles and Melissa Fletcher, the innkeepers of The China Clipper Inn, serve this creamy quiche with oven-roasted potatoes, sausage links and a fresh fruit salad. It's perfect for breakfast or brunch and is full of flavor, like so many of The China Clipper Inn's breakfast dishes.

6 large eggs

1 cup heavy cream

1 tsp. garlic powder

½ tsp. paprika

1 tsp. kosher salt

½ tsp. ground white pepper

1 cup sharp cheddar cheese, grated

½ cup parmesan cheese, grated

½ cup smoked gouda cheese, grated

1 9-inch pie crust, unbaked (store bought or homemade)

¼ cup fresh chives, minced

SERVES 6 – 8

EASIEST

Preheat oven to 350 degrees. In a large bowl, whisk together eggs, cream, garlic powder, paprika, salt, and white pepper. Stir in cheeses. Pour mixture into unbaked pie shell. Sprinkle chives on top. Bake until quiche is lightly golden and set in the center when the pan is gently pushed, about 40 - 45 minutes. If the crust is browning too quickly, cover with foil to prevent burning.

Remove from oven and let stand for 5 - 10 minutes before serving. Cut into 6 or 8 slices and serve warm or at room temperature.

SERVING SUGGESTION:
Sprinkle with fresh chives.

STEAK & EGGS

THE ESSEX RESORT AND SPA • ESSEX, VERMONT

The Essex Resort, Vermont's Culinary Resort, introduced this Steak & Eggs dish on their 2019 Spring breakfast menu. They wanted to achieve a fulfilling steak and eggs dish, but with a twist. This recipe features a beautifully seared steak with lots of fresh pepper to give it a fruity, peppery taste. That, combined with the rich eggs, fresh flavor of wilted greens and acidity from their Batch 7 Sauce, makes this a deeply fulfilling meal.

4 oz. New York strip

2 large local free-range eggs, cooked to liking

½ cup local red Russian kale, stems removed and chopped

¼ cup Batch 7 Sauce, see recipe

1 slice sourdough, ½" thick

1 Tbsp. pepper, freshly and coarsely ground

1 pinch kosher salt

¼ cup olive oil

Fresh herbs, minced

SERVES 1

Dry steak with paper towel and rest at room temperature for 15 – 30 minutes. Toast and grind fresh peppercorns – use black peppercorns or a peppercorn mixture, which gives a fruitier flavor. Season steak with pepper and salt. Sear steak in a sauté pan or on a grill to preferred temperature. Remove and let rest.

Quickly sauté kale in a hot pan with a drizzle of olive oil; the greens should still have a bite to them. Season to taste. Cook eggs to liking, sunny side is recommended.

Season sourdough with salt and brush with olive oil and sear. Slice rested steak. Assemble dish with sourdough on the bottom, add kale then sliced steak fanned-out evenly. Drizzle with Batch 7 Sauce. Finally, add the eggs on top with a sprinkling of fresh herbs.

SERVING SUGGESTION:
Serve with breakfast potatoes or garden-fresh vegetables.

BATCH 7 SAUCE

½ cup barbeque sauce (Richard's Vermont-made is recommended)

2 Tbsp. sriracha sauce

2 Tbsp. ketchup

1 Tbsp. whole grain mustard

Whisk together all ingredients. This can be made ahead.

TAOS TAMALE EGG BAKE

OLD TAOS GUESTHOUSE INN • TAOS, NEW MEXICO

Nestled amid a grove of stately old Taos cottonwoods and spruce, Bob and Cady Aspinwall's inn on 7.5 acres overlooking Taos began as an adobe home built over 200 years ago. This farmer's home turned artist's estate was lovingly restored into a Southwestern traditional bed and breakfast hacienda with a rich and colorful history.

8 eggs

1 cup half and half

¼ cup cilantro, chopped

½ cup hot salsa

8 tamales, store bought or home-make a favorite recipe and cut in thirds

2 cups medium cheddar cheese, shredded

Cilantro, for garnish

Sour cream, for garnish

SERVES 12

EASIEST

Preheat oven to 350 degrees. Grease a 9 x 13 baking dish. Place tamales in baking dish and cover with cheese. Mix together eggs, half and half, cilantro and salsa. Pour over tamales. Bake for 45 minutes. Rest for at least 15 minutes before serving.

SERVING SUGGESTION:
If individual servings appeal, like the photograph, use 4-inch ramekins and divide the ingredients equally amongst the ramekins.

SAVORY BREAD PUDDING

LIBERTY HILL FARM & INN • ROCHESTER, VERMONT

Liberty Hill Farm & Inn is a Gold Barn Award member of the Vermont Fresh Network, given in recognition of chefs who've cultivated exceptional partnerships with Vermont farmers. Beth Kennett's culinary handiwork has been glowingly written up in Gourmet, Travel and Leisure, Yankee, Family Fun, The New York Times, Boston Globe, Vermont Life, *and seen on* Good Morning America, Boston Chronicle *and more.*

1 Tbsp. olive oil or butter

1 cup red onion, diced

1 cup mushrooms, sliced

1 cup red bell pepper, diced

1 large bunch kale or spinach, stems removed and torn in pieces

3 garlic cloves, minced

8 cups bread (your choice: whole grain, challah, brioche), 1-inch cubes

1 ½ cups Cabot seriously sharp cheddar cheese, shredded

6 large eggs

3 cups whole milk

Salt and pepper to taste

S E R V E S 8 -1 0

SERVING SUGGESTION:
Enjoy this modern twist on a grandmother's recipe, as Beth describes her creations.

EASIEST

Butter a 13 x 9 casserole dish and set aside (or use a 10-inch souffle dish).

Heat olive oil or butter in skillet over medium heat. Add onions, mushrooms, peppers, and cook for 5 minutes, stirring often. Add kale and garlic and stir for one minute. Season with salt and pepper, then remove from heat and set aside. Place half the bread cubes in prepared dish, top with half vegetable mixture and half cheese. Repeat with remaining bread cubes, vegetable mixture, and cheese.

Whisk eggs in large bowl, then whisk in milk. Pour egg mixture over bread in baking dish. Cover with wrap, press down slightly to help egg mixture soak into bread. Refrigerate several hours or overnight.

When ready to bake, preheat oven to 350 degrees. Uncover and bake for 45-60 minutes or until golden brown and a wooden pick inserted in center comes out clean.

BEET-CURED SALMON
with Goat Cheese Mousse, Pickled Fennel and Crostini

EDSON HILL • CHEF JASON BISSELL • STOWE, VERMONT

Indulge in a sensational meal prepared by Chef Jason Bissell and the Edson Hill culinary team whose creations feature a modern approach to classic New England fare. The Dining Room at Edson Hill provides an elegant backdrop for a truly unforgettable culinary experience with its intimate ambiance and fish bowl views of picturesque grounds from nearly every angle. When eating at the renowned Edson Hill, you will be delighted with the creativity and masterful execution of the dishes.

10 oz. salmon, skinless

½ baguette, thinly sliced on bias

Olive oil

Goat Cheese Mousse, see recipe

Pickled Fennel, see recipe

Beet Cure, see recipe

Capers, for garnish

SERVES 2

 MORE DIFFICULT

Place half Beet Cure in a small glass pan, place salmon on top of the cure, put remainder of Beet Cure on salmon, wrap pan in plastic and cure for 48 hours. After 48 hours, rinse salmon and pat dry, slice thinly.

When ready to assemble, place baguette slices on baking sheet and drizzle with olive oil. Bake at 350 degrees for 8 - 10 minutes. Remove slices from oven and assemble by adding dollops of Goat Cheese Mousse to the plate, alternating baguette slices and salmon slices, then arranging Pickled Fennel on top.

SERVING SUGGESTION:
Garnish this dish with capers.

BEET CURE

1 red beet, grated

¼ cup sugar

½ cup salt

½ tsp. ground juniper

½ tsp. ground coriander

½ tsp. ground black pepper

1 orange, zested

Mix all ingredients together.

GOAT CHEESE MOUSSE

2 oz. goat cheese

2 oz. cream cheese, softened

1 Tbsp. honey

½ lemon, juiced

Mix all ingredients until incorporated.

PICKLED FENNEL

1 fennel bulb, finely julienned

½ cup cider vinegar

3 Tbsp. white sugar

1 pinch salt

2 star anise pods

2 clove pods

Simmer vinegar, sugar, salt, star anise, and cloves. Pour hot liquid over fennel and set for 48 hours in refrigerator.

IDAHO SHORT RIB & POTATO HASH

SHORE LODGE • MCCALL, IDAHO

For an easy two-meal preparation, double this recipe for dinner, and use leftovers for breakfast the following morning. Though short ribs are used for this recipe, any leftover braised meat such as pot roast, lamb shank, or osso buco can be used.

Braised Short Ribs, meat removed from bone and diced into ¾" cubes, see recipe

1 red onion, peeled and julienned

1 yellow bell pepper, cored and seeds removed, julienned

1 red bell pepper, cored and seeds removed, julienned

6 - 8 red potatoes, skin on, diced into ¾" cubes

3 - 4 oz. reserved braising liquid

2 - 3 Tbsp. clarified butter

8 eggs, cooked to liking

Kosher salt and ground black pepper

Hollandaise Sauce, see recipe

Italian parsley and radishes, for garnish

SERVES 4

In a medium saucepan, add potatoes and cover with cold water, then season liberally with salt and place on high heat until boiling. Reduce heat and simmer for 4 - 5 minutes, or until potatoes are tender but not mushy. Strain potatoes and cool. Place a large cast iron skillet over high heat. Add butter and evenly coat bottom of pan, add potatoes and diced short rib meat, stirring with a wooden spoon to prevent sticking. When meat and potatoes have browned, add onions and peppers, seasoning lightly with salt and pepper. Stir until onions and peppers have begun to caramelize. Deglaze pan with reserved braising liquid, and reduce until the pan is almost dry again. Remove from heat and portion into four bowls. Top each portion with two eggs cooked to liking, drizzle liberally with Hollandaise Sauce.

HOLLANDAISE SAUCE

3 egg yolks

12 oz. clarified butter

1 Tbsp. lemon juice

1 tsp. Worcestershire

½ tsp. Tabasco

1 Tbsp. whole grain mustard

Kosher salt to taste

In saucepan, heat clarified butter until liquefied and hot, then reserve. In a metal or heat-resistant ceramic bowl, combine egg yolks, lemon juice, Worcestershire, mustard, and Tabasco. Place bowl over double boiler on low heat, whisk constantly to combine and warm; do not let eggs scramble. Remove from heat when mixture is warm, but not hot. Whisking quickly to emulsify, drizzle clarified butter in, slowly at first, so that it incorporates into the eggs without separating. Sauce will begin to thicken, if it becomes too thick, use drops of warm water to adjust consistency. Season to taste with kosher salt. The final result will be a sauce that heavily coats a spoon, but not as thick as an aioli.

BRAISED SHORT RIBS

4 lbs. bone-in beef short ribs

2 - 3 Tbsp. vegetable oil

1 yellow onion, peeled and large diced

1 large carrot, peeled and large diced

2 ribs celery, large diced

1 head garlic, peeled

½ oz. fresh thyme, whole with stems

1 oz. fresh rosemary, whole with stems

6 bay leaves

12 oz. can tomato paste

1 cup red wine

2 quarts beef stock or broth

Kosher salt and ground black pepper

Preheat convection oven to 300 degrees. Place short ribs on sheet pan and season liberally on all sides with salt and pepper. Rest at room temperature for 30 - 45 minutes. Heat oil on high in medium-sized roasting pan with lid, sear short ribs, meat side down first, until darkly caramelized, about 7 - 8 minutes per side. Remove short ribs from pan. In same pan, add onions, carrots, celery, and whole garlic cloves. Season with salt and pepper. Stir regularly to caramelize on all sides. Add thyme, rosemary, bay leaves, and tomato paste. Stir constantly until herbs are fragrant and tomato paste begins to caramelize. Deglaze pan with red wine. Reduce wine by half, then return short ribs to pan, adding enough beef stock to just cover the meat, leaving the bones exposed. Cover with lid or aluminum foil. Cook in oven 2 ½ - 3 hours, or until meat is tender and beginning to pull away from bone. Once cooked, remove ribs from braising liquid and chill 2 - 3 hours, or overnight. Strain vegetables from sauce; reserve liquid.

SERVING SUGGESTION:
Garnish with fresh Italian parsley and sliced radishes.

HAPPY COOKER OLD FASHIONED THREE-CHEESE QUICHE

THE HISTORIC HAPPY COOKER • GEORGETOWN, COLORADO

Georgetown, Colorado sits at an elevation of 8,530 feet and is nestled in the mountains near the upper end of the valley of Clear Creek County. Although a small town today, the town was a historic center of the mining industry in Colorado during the late 19th century, earning the nickname "Silver Queen of Colorado". In a building dating back to 1898, The Historic Happy Cooker is considered a long-time icon in the town of Georgetown (going on 45 years now) and while many of the recipes have been kept in the family for years, the restaurant is generously sharing the Three-Cheese Quiche recipe.

2 ½ cups eggs, beaten

1 cup heavy whipping cream

1 cup feta cheese, crumbled

1 cup goat cheese, crumbled

1 cup sharp cheddar cheese, shredded

Salt and pepper

Pie shell, store bought or home-make a favorite recipe, optional

SERVES 6 - 8

Preheat oven to 350 degrees. In a large bowl, combine eggs, whipping cream, ½ of the sharp cheddar cheese, and all of the feta and goat cheeses. Pour into a greased 9-inch deep-dish pie plate. If preferred, make this with a pie crust. Perforate the pie crust before pouring the mixture into the shell. Sprinkle with remaining ½ of the sharp cheddar cheese. Bake 45 - 50 minutes or until a knife inserted in the center comes out clean. Let stand 10 minutes before cutting.

SERVING SUGGESTION:
Serve alongside a fresh salad.

GOOD OL' BOY OMELETTE

SOMERS BAY CAFE • SOMERS, MONTANA

Somers Bay Cafe is located in the old Somers State Bank building, built in 1905. In it's hey-day, Somers was a major port, milltown and tie yard. The cafe is a mini-museum of old-time Somers, displaying historical photos and artifacts on the walls.

3 eggs

1 tsp. butter

1 cup sharp cheddar cheese, shredded

2 slices bacon, cooked and crumbled

¼ cup sausage, cooked and crumbled

¼ cup ham, cooked and chopped

2 Tbsp. tomato, diced

2 Tbsp. onion, chopped and sautéed

2 Tbsp. green pepper, chopped and sautéed

Pinch salt and pepper

SERVES 1

EASIEST

In a small bowl, beat eggs, salt and pepper. In a 10-inch nonstick skillet, melt butter over medium heat, rotating pan to coat bottom. Add egg mixture, gently lift edges with a spatula and tilt pan so uncooked portion flows underneath. Cook for 3 - 4 minutes, or until just set. Sprinkle filling ingredients evenly onto half of omelette. Fold omelette in half. Cook for 1 minute or until cheese is melted.

SERVING SUGGESTION:
Garnish the top of the omelette with any leftover filling ingredients.

COUNTRY FRIED QUAIL BENEDICT

THE YELLOWSTONE CLUB • CHEF ROB WALTZ • BIG SKY, MONTANA

Yellowstone Club's superior amenities, Montana charm, and amazing natural beauty present an incomparable venue for mountain living, year-round recreation, and cherished family traditions. Explore the spectacular beauty of the world's only private ski and golf community while enjoying the benefits of membership in this exclusive one-of-a-kind club.

Tomato and Herb Hollandaise, see recipe

½ cup flour

Brioche loaf, sliced

2 eggs

Grapeseed or canola oil

3 Tbsp. white vinegar

Salt and black pepper

1 quail, semi-boned

3 green onions, for garnish

SERVES 1 – 2

 MORE DIFFICULT Season flour with salt and pepper. Lightly dredge quail in flour and pan fry in oil for two minutes per side. Keep warm in oven.

Add vinegar and a liberal amount of salt into boiling pot of water. Stir creating a small whirlpool and add eggs. Slowly poach for 7 minutes. Toast or grill brioche slices. Assemble by placing brioche on a plate with quail on top, then poached eggs, and finally drizzle Tomato and Herb Hollandaise.

For an advanced garnish, use 1 additional quail breast and place between wax paper, pound very thin until almost translucent, lightly flour and wrap around a 2-inch circular cutter and refrigerate. Use a large pot with 2-inches of oil, gently lower in the ring mold with quail breast wrapped around the outside and fry until golden brown. Use this circular piece to highlight your plate.

SERVING SUGGESTION:

Garnish dish with charred green onions and pan-fried diced potatoes and parsnips.

TOMATO AND HERB HOLLANDAISE

3 egg yolks

2 tsp. lemon juice

2 dashes Tabasco

1 cup clarified butter

Black pepper, freshly cracked

1 tsp. tomato, chopped

1 pinch fresh chervil

In stainless steel bowl, whisk yolks with 1 Tbsp. water, lemon juice, and Tabasco over a mildly boiling pot of water until mixture turns lemon yellow and thickens slightly. Remove from heat and slowly whisk in butter, 1 Tbsp. warm water, pepper, tomato and chervil. Reserve in a warm spot until plating.

RANCHERO OMELETTE

BARDENAY • BOISE, IDAHO

At Bardenay, it all comes together in a uniquely Idaho atmosphere, creating an experience to be relished. As the nation's first restaurant distillery, Bardenay set an industry precedent by combining a full service restaurant and bar with a distillery. With 3 locations and each specializing in distilling different spirits, the Boise Bardenay produces ginger rum, amber rum, and still aging dark rum and rye whiskey.

1 lb. rotisserie chicken, shredded

3 poblano peppers, roasted and diced

2 roma tomatoes, sliced ¼" thick

1 cup artichoke hearts, from a can or jar and quartered

1 cup sour cream

1 lb. cheddar cheese, shredded

1 lb. mozzarella cheese, shredded

7 Crepes, see recipe

Salsa, for garnish

SERVES 8

MORE DIFFICULT

In a 9"x 3" spring form pan, layer in the following way:

(1) two overlapping crepes, ¼ cup sour cream smear, ½ the amount of chicken, ½ the amount of poblano peppers, ¼ the amount of cheddar and mozzarella.

(2) two overlapping crepes, ¼ cup sour cream smear, tomatoes, artichoke hearts, ¼ the amount of cheddar and mozzarella.

(3) two overlapping crepes, ¼ cup sour cream smear, ½ the amount of chicken, ½ the amount of poblano peppers, ¼ the amount of cheddar and mozzarella.

(4) final crepe, ¼ cup sour cream smear, ¼ the amount of cheddar and mozzarella.

Wrap with plastic and press with a weight to help set evenly for one hour in refrigerator. Bake uncovered at 350 degrees in oven for 30 minutes, and make sure the cheese is melted. Let rest 5 minutes before slicing.

SERVING SUGGESTION:
Serve an ample slice with salsa.

CREPES

8 extra-large eggs

¼ cup heavy whipping cream

1 Tbsp. Spike Original Seasoning

2 Tbsp. cilantro, chopped

MAKES 7 CREPES

Combine all crepe ingredients and scramble. Heat a small pan (8-10") over medium-high heat. Use a light amount of pan spray and gently swirl approximately 6 oz. mixture with a little shake to cook egg as high up pan as possible. Continue to roll out until egg mixture is completely set on one side. Once edges start browning and no more loose egg appears, flip once to set the other side. Slide out and stack.

THE BREAKFAST ENCHILADA

EAST SIDE BAKE SHOP • MAMMOTH LAKES, CALIFORNIA

Elizabeth McGuire, East Side Bake Shop owner and baker, derived this recipe from her mother's cheese enchiladas, which is a story that warms her heart with each retelling. While this recipe is utterly simple, it continues to impress. Elizabeth believes that there is something innate within us that likes food cooked-up and presented in a cast iron. Whether satisfying an inner-pioneer pull or merely a hearty hunger, The Breakfast Enchilada will make taste buds happy and fill a skier's belly!

4 cups cottage cheese

4 ½ cups jack and cheddar cheese, shredded

6 oz. black olives, minced

10 – 12 corn tortillas

2 ½ cups medium-hot chunky salsa

8 eggs

SERVES 6 – 8

SERVING SUGGESTION: Enjoy a slice before a day on the mountain!

EASIEST

Preheat oven to 350 degrees. Combine cottage cheese, 4 cups shredded cheese mix and olives in a large bowl. Line the bottom of a 12-inch cast iron skillet with 5-6 overlapping corn tortillas. Spoon cottage cheese mixture on top of corn tortillas. Place another 5-6 overlapping corn tortillas atop the cottage cheese mix. Press down to evenly distribute cottage cheese mixture in between two tortilla layers. Top with salsa and completely cover tortillas below. Sprinkle remaining shredded cheese on top. Crack and evenly disperse 8 raw eggs around the top of the cast iron casserole.

Bake uncovered for 35 - 45 minutes, until the egg whites are set. Cool the casserole before slicing.

CRAB SALAD EGGS BENEDICT
with Three Citrus Hollandaise Sauce

SUNDANCE MOUNTAIN RESORT • SUNDANCE, UTAH

The Sundance Mountain Resort has a food philosophy: Food As Art. This belief combined with the thought that dining is communal is showcased at the multitude of dining options at Sundance, where guests are welcomed to enjoy dining integrated with nature.

2 eggs, poached

1 English muffin, sliced and toasted

½ cup Crab Salad, see recipe

4 Tbsp. Three Citrus Hollandaise Sauce, see recipe

4 Tbsp. Chives, minced for garnish

SERVES 1

SERVING SUGGESTION:
Garnish with minced chives.

 Add toasted muffins to a serving dish, top with Crab Salad and poached eggs, and spoon Three Citrus Hollandaise Sauce on top.

CRAB SALAD

1 lb. lump crab, canned

½ cup red pepper, ¼" diced

½ cup red onion, ¼" diced

½ cup celery, ¼" diced

¼ cup mayo

1 Tbsp. whole grain mustard

Salt and pepper to taste

Lemon zest to taste

MAKES 1 QUART

Gently fold together all ingredients and season with salt, pepper and lemon zest to taste. Refrigerate until ready for use.

THREE CITRUS HOLLANDAISE SAUCE

¾ cup hot clarified butter

5 egg yolks

1 orange, juiced and zested

1 lime, juiced and zested

1 lemon, juiced and zested

4 dashes Tabasco

Salt to taste

MAKES 2 CUPS

Add juices, zests, egg yolks, and Tabasco to a warm mixing bowl. Whisk to incorporate ingredients. Slowly stream in hot clarified butter while vigorously whisking. Continue process quickly until all the butter is used or until thickness is achieved. Season to taste with salt. Cover and hold in a warm area until ready to use.

POLISH PILE

KATY'S CAFÉ • CHEF KATY HERBACH • ELLICOTTVILLE, NEW YORK

Owner and chef of Katy's Café, Katy Herbach was raised on her mother's pierogies, so upon opening the café, she started making them for Dyngus day, which is Easter Monday celebrated in Poland. These treats were so beloved that Katy created a recipe to feature the pierogies on the regular menu. The recommended flavors for the pierogies in this dish range from potato and onion, farmers cheese or sauerkraut. Pierogies can be homemade or store bought and can be found in the freezer section of most grocery stores and with the fresh pastas, in some specialty markets.

20 red potatoes, cooked and diced

1 lb. polish sausage (fresh or smoked), chopped

12 - 15 pierogies

8 oz. jar roasted red peppers, diced

1 yellow onion, sautéed

½ – 1 cup sauerkraut

½ cup butter, divided

8 - 12 eggs

1 ½ tsp. Cajun seasoning

1 tsp. garlic salt

1 ½ tsp. black pepper

1 tsp. paprika

8 - 12 oz. cheddar cheese, shredded

SERVES 4 - 6

MORE DIFFICULT

Melt half the butter in a frying pan. Add cooked and diced potatoes; season with garlic salt, Cajun seasoning, black pepper, and paprika. Cook until potatoes begin to brown. Add sausage, sautéed onions, sauerkraut and roasted red peppers. Cook mixture for another 5 - 10 minutes. Add cheddar cheese. In a separate pan, melt half the butter and sauté pierogies until lightly golden on each side. When finished, plate potato mixture with pierogies on top. The other half of the butter can be used to make over easy eggs, which is suggested. Add eggs to the top the pile.

SERVING SUGGESTION:
Top the Polish Pile with a sprinkle of shredded cheddar cheese.

CREAM EGGS

SNOWBERRY INN BED & BREAKFAST • CHEF ANDREA BURK • EDEN, UTAH

Chef and Innkeeper at Snowberry Inn Bed & Breakfast, Andrea Burk's vast career experience lends itself to the success of Snowberry Inn. After culinary school and receiving a degree in business finance, she followed her dreams of becoming a business owner with the Snowberry Inn. Andrea enhances her guest's experience with her diverse background – even her adventurous spirit, her love for the mountains and passion for skiing from being a ski racer for Snowbasin brings joy.

2 Tbsp. unsalted butter, divided

3 cups hash browns, frozen and shredded

¾ cup shredded cheese

¾ cup cream

12 eggs

1 tsp. salt

½ tsp. black pepper, freshly cracked

SERVES 6

Preheat oven to 400 degrees. Butter 6 ramekins with ⅛ tsp. softened butter each. In remaining butter, sauté hash browns to soften. Spoon hash browns into ramekins and add a dash of salt to each. Sprinkle cheese on top of hash browns. Drizzle cream evenly among cheese and hash browns, add another dash of salt. Crack two eggs on top and season with salt and pepper to taste. Set on a sheet pan on the bottom rack of oven and bake for 30 – 35 minutes or until eggs set.

SERVING SUGGESTION:
Serve immediately with toast, bacon, sausage and fresh fruit.

VEGETARIAN FRITTATA

THE SWEET SPOT • WAITSFIELD, VERMONT

The Sweet Spot is inspired by taking classics and putting a twist on them. They hand-make from scratch as much as possible right down to the ginger syrup in their cocktails to the caramel in their ice cream. The menu changes frequently to ensure fresh, seasonal dishes are always served.

3 Tbsp. ghee (clarified butter)

3 russet potatoes, quartered and sliced

5 cups eggs, scrambled (approximately 20 eggs)

1 cup heavy cream

1 Tbsp. garlic, chopped

1 Tbsp. onion, chopped

1 cup cheddar, shredded

4 cups kale, chopped

¾ cup chevre

¾ cup cherry tomatoes, roasted

¼ cup basil, chopped

Salt and pepper

Basil, for garnish

SERVES 6

SERVING SUGGESTION:
Sprinkle some extra fresh basil on a generous slice.

Preheat oven to 350 degrees. On the stovetop in a 12-inch seasoned cast iron pan, heat ghee. Add potatoes, season with salt and pepper. Cook potatoes until brown and tender. While potatoes are cooking, whisk together eggs, cream, garlic, onion, and cheddar. Season with salt and pepper. When potatoes are done, turn off heat and add kale. Add egg mixture and gently mix the potatoes, kale and egg mixture.

The cast iron pan should be filled to the top. If it is not, add more scrambled eggs. Or, extra egg mixture may be remaining depending on the depth of the pan.

Add chevre, tomatoes, and basil. With steady hands put the full pan in the oven. Bake for approximately 1 hour. The frittata is done when it does not jiggle when you shake the handle of the pan.

SHRIMP CAKE BENEDICT

BUFFALO CAFÉ • CHEF ANDY MAETZOLD • WHITEFISH, MONTANA

Rich, flavorful, and fresh - the Shrimp Cake Benedict is the perfect way to indulge during any ski trip! The shrimp cakes first appeared as an appetizer on Buffalo Café's dinner menu, but Chef Andy decided to branch-out and try it for breakfast. The Shrimp Cake Benny was quickly established as a new local favorite and a staple on the brunch menu. "We are making fresh hollandaise from scratch throughout the entire day at "The Buff" and for us its all about taking the time and making a nice smooth sauce that can't be rushed. When it comes to choosing the right shrimp for your recipe, we never compromise on choosing a wild caught product," Chef Andy proudly states.

1 lb. raw shrimp, peeled and deveined

¼ cup capers

1 Tbsp. shallot, chopped

¼ cup red bell pepper, chopped

½ cup mayo

½ Tbsp. salt

½ Tbsp. dill

Splash lemon juice

1 ½ cups panko

6 – 8 English muffins, toasted

12 – 16 eggs, poached

Hollandaise Sauce, see recipe

SERVES 6 - 8

SERVING SUGGESTION:
This pairs perfectly with a mimosa!

MORE DIFFICULT

In a food processor, add shrimp, capers, shallots, peppers, mayo, salt, dill, and lemon juice. Process lightly, making sure not to over mix into a paste. Add half of panko amount until mixture becomes thick.

Add remaining panko into a mixing bowl. Make ¼ cup balls of shrimp cake mix and roll in panko until coated. Flatten between parchment paper into 2-inch diameters. Cook shrimp cakes in a large skillet over medium-high heat until golden brown.

To create the Benedict, serve finished shrimp cakes atop toasted English muffin halves with poached eggs. Top with Hollandaise Sauce.

HOLLANDAISE SAUCE

12 - 15 egg yolks

3 Tbsp. lemon juice

¼ tsp. white pepper

½ tsp. Dijon mustard

1 lb. butter, melted

Combine egg yolks, lemon juice, white pepper and Dijon mustard in a stainless steel mixing bowl. Whip over a hot water bath, until thick and light. Very slowly, whip in melted butter. Finished sauce should be thick but pourable.

SHAKSHUKA

THE EATING ESTABLISHMENT • CHEF BRENDAN KAWAKAMI • PARK CITY, UTAH

Opened in 1972, The Eating Establishment has been a beloved diner to three generations of locals and visitors to Park City. In 2017, The Eating Establishment was purchased by a small group of local yahoos and spruced-up; in this case, adding a bar is the definition of "spruced-up". Chef Brendan Kawakami's menu preserves the original spirit of a 'breakfast all day' restaurant while adding new comfort food elements and bringing craft cocktails of Bar X and a portion of the beer list from Beer Bar (the sister businesses in Salt Lake City) up the mountain. Dig in, drink up!

1 cup spicy tomato sauce

¼ cup potatoes, cooked and diced or shredded

¼ cup feta cheese, crumbled

¼ cup kale, torn

2 eggs

S ERVES 1

EASIEST

Heat tomato sauce in skillet, add potatoes, kale and ½ of feta cheese. Top with whole eggs, making sure to keep the yolk intact. Cover the skillet. Cook until egg is at preferred temperature. Multiply this recipe to serve as many hearty appetites as desired, merely increase the size of the pan.

SERVING SUGGESTION:
Garnish with remaining feta cheese and fresh herbs. Serve with toast.

BRUNCH BURGER

HOME TEAM BBQ • ASPEN, COLORADO

Home Team BBQ is a casual restaurant set at the base of Buttermilk Mountain in Aspen, Colorado, however the mothership's Southern roots were first established in Charleston, South Carolina in 2006. The menu is built on a foundation of smoked meats and Southern staples developed by former "white tablecloth" chefs, with dishes sourced from the freshest, quality products. This certainly does not exclude the items on the brunch menu, such as "Fiery Ron's Brunch Burger," which can definitely separate the men from the boys on Sunday morning. Home Team BBQ's brunch burger starts with 100% ground brisket, a spoonful of harissa mayo to add the perfect richness and spice, topped with a farm fresh egg for a 'sunny side up' flavor, then American cheese and house-made smoked bacon on a lightly toasted brioche bun.

2 4 oz. ground brisket patties

2 slices bacon, smoked

2 slices American cheese

1 Tbsp. Harissa Mayo, see recipe

1 sunny side up egg

1 brioche bun, 3 ½" round

1 tsp. oil

SERVES 1

Preheat oven to 350 degrees. On medium heat in a 10 - 12-inch cast iron pan or griddle, cook strips of bacon until desired crispness. Set bacon aside. Clean cast iron pan, heat ½ tsp. oil on medium heat. Cook patties until seared on both sides then add cheese slices to each patty. In oven, lightly toast brioche bun on a cookie sheet face down for 2 - 3 minutes. Using a nonstick 6 - 8-inch sauté pan on low to medium heat, add remaining oil and carefully crack egg to avoid breaking yolk. Once the white is fully cooked, turn heat off. Spread Harissa Mayo on bottom bun, add both patties, place two strips of bacon on top of patties, and then place sunny side up egg over bacon. Add more Harissa Mayo to top bun and carefully place atop egg.

SERVING SUGGESTION:
Remember to squeeze the burger to break the yolk. Enjoy the burst of messy-morning deliciousness!

HARISSA MAYO

32 oz. jar Dukes Mayo

2 Tbsp. harissa paste (DEA brand recommended)

8 cloves garlic

Salt and pepper to taste

Using a microplane, or very fine cheese grater, mince garlic. Combine all ingredients in a bowl or food processor and mix until harissa paste is fully incorporated. Season with salt and pepper and refrigerate up to 7 days.

LOBSTER EGGS BENEDICT

MIRROR LAKE INN • LAKE PLACID, NEW YORK

In 2018, among other awards, Mirror Lake Inn was voted "#2 Waterfront Hotel and #1 Lakefront Hotel in the U.S." by USA Today's Reader's Choice Awards, "Best Hotel in New York State" by Conde' Nast Traveler, and one of the "8 Luxurious Hotels on the World's Most Tranquil Lakes" by ArchitecturalDigest.com.

2 whole eggs

4 oz. lobster meat, poached

2 English muffins

Hollandaise Sauce, see recipe

SERVES 1 – 2

Toast English muffins, poach eggs, and warm lobster in buttered water. Assemble by placing English muffin halves on a plate, place eggs on top, drizzle with Hollandaise Sauce and garnish with warmed lobster.

HOLLANDAISE SAUCE

1 cup salted butter

2 large egg yolks

1 Tbsp. lemon juice

Frank's Red Hot Sauce

Salt

Melt butter in a small sauce pan and set to the side, keeping it warm. In a metal bowl, whisk egg yolks, lemon juice, and 1 Tbsp. water. Over pot of simmering water, gently whisk egg yolk mixture until it begins to thicken, making sure the bottom of the bowl is not touching the water. Drizzle in butter. Season to taste with salt and Frank's Red Hot Sauce.

SERVING SUGGESTION:

Enjoy the decadence knowing the recipe comes from an award-winning location.

WILD GAME CHORIZO AREPA

MONTAGE DEER VALLEY • CHEF CHRISTIAN OJEDA • PARK CITY, UTAH

Arepa is the daily bread of Venezuela handed down generations from the Timoto-Cuicas, a local tribe. Made of white cornmeal, water and salt, the dough is formed into a flat, round, unleavened patty. Chef Christian utilizes his distinctive blend of classic European, progressive American and unique Southwestern culinary expertise at Montage Deer Valley.

2 lbs. ground turkey

1 lb. ground venison

1 lb. ground bison

6 Tbsp. chili flakes (guajillo, chipotle, and/or ancho)

2 Tbsp. salt

1 tsp. ground coriander

1 tsp. ground cumin

1 ½ tsp. oregano

2 tsp. garlic powder

⅓ cup cider vinegar

3 Tbsp. oil of your choice

Salt and pepper to taste

Salsa Verde, see recipe

Arepa Cornmeal Cake, see recipe

1 egg, cooked sunny side up

Caramelized onions, peppers and spinach, for garnish

SERVES 4 - 6

SERVING SUGGESTION:
This creative dish is also splendid topped with caramelized onions, peppers and spinach before adding the sunny side up egg.

Add chili flakes, salt, coriander, cumin, oregano and garlic powder to food processor or blender. Pulse until spices are evenly mixed. With your hands, knead together meats, spices and vinegar. Cover and refrigerate overnight to develop flavor. Knead meat again to thoroughly mix the seasoning in the meat. In a medium saucepan, with 3 Tbsp. oil, add wild game chorizo, and sauté until fully cooked, approximately 10 minutes. Add Salsa Verde to pan, simmer for 5 more minutes. Season with salt and pepper to taste. Place wild game chorizo on the bottom of the plate then add Arepa Cornmeal Cake on top. Top with sunny side up egg.

SALSA VERDE

10 tomatillos, husks removed and washed

½ yellow onion, peeled and rough chopped

1 jalapeno, stem and seeds removed

2 garlic cloves

½ lime, juiced

¼ bunch fresh cilantro

Salt and pepper to taste

Preheat oven to 400 degrees. On a small sheet pan, roast tomatillos until tender, 10 - 15 minutes. Remove tomatillos from oven and completely cool, before blending. Blend all ingredients until smooth. Season with salt and pepper to taste.

AREPA CORNMEAL CAKE

1 ¼ cups white cornmeal (P.A.N. Brand, found in most Spanish markets)

1 cup water

1 tsp. salt

1 quart fry oil

Pour water in a bowl with salt. Gradually add corn meal and knead until mixture is a smooth consistency. In a small pot, add 1 quart of fry oil, preheat to 350 degrees. Slowly add a circular-shaped cornmeal cake and cook until crispy and golden brown, 5 minutes.

WILD WOOD'S EGGS ROCKEFELLER

WILD WOOD PACIFIC BISTRO • WHISTLER, BRITISH COLUMBIA, CANADA

Operated by longtime Whistler locals, the Wild Wood Pacific Bistro is passionate about what they offer: fresh west coast flavors, friendly mountain-style service and a cozy atmosphere; there is no better place to start or finish a day.

1 bunch spinach, fresh or frozen

1 cup white onions, ¼" diced

2 Tbsp. olive oil

2 tsp. garlic, minced

¼ cup 35% heavy cream

Salt

Freshly ground black pepper

2 English muffins, halved

4 eggs

2 Tbsp. vinegar

Hollandaise sauce, store bought or home-make a favorite recipe

Pinch of cayenne pepper

SERVES **2**

EASIEST

Wash fresh spinach or thaw frozen spinach and drain. Sauté onions, lightly seasoned with salt and freshly ground black pepper, in olive oil until softened and turning golden. Add garlic; cook 1 minute. Add spinach and toss to combine. Cook for 5 minutes, stirring occasionally, until liquid has evaporated. Incorporate cream and cook until reduced and thickened. Keep warm.

Boil salted water, add vinegar and poach eggs. When eggs are just set – yolks should be soft to medium, remove with slotted spoon. Drain eggs on paper towels. Toast English muffins until slightly crisp. Place eggs on a bed of creamed spinach atop each English muffin half then finish with hollandaise over top. Sprinkle with cayenne for garnish.

SERVING SUGGESTION:

As this recipe serves 2, enjoy with one of your favorite people.

PORTOBELLO BENEDICT

PERRY'S • KETCHUM, IDAHO

With this Benedict, preparation is the key to executing this breadless, vegetarian variation on the classic Eggs Benedict. At Perry's, the mushrooms are marinated for 1 – 2 hours before cooking on the grill. Keith and Paula Perry have been serving Sun Valley for decades, so they know what they're advocating – timing is everything!

8 Portobello mushrooms, gills removed from underside with a spoon

Portobello Marinade, see recipe

Fresh spinach

Hollandaise sauce, store bought or a favorite homemade recipe

8 eggs

Avocado, for garnish

Tomato, for garnish

SERVES 4

MORE DIFFICULT

Marinate mushrooms in Portobello Marinade for 1 – 2 hours.

Heat hollandaise sauce and keep warm. Simmer water in a pot for poaching eggs. Remove mushrooms from marinade and pat dry with a paper towel. Grill mushrooms on medium heat, 5 minutes per side. Add eggs to lightly boiling water for 4 minutes. Lightly wilt fresh spinach in a pan, about 1 - 2 minutes. Place mushrooms on plate, as the base. Add spinach on top followed by poached eggs and top with hollandaise. Add a dash of paprika for color. * The photo shows a deconstructed example of the Portobello Benedict.

SERVING SUGGESTION:
Avocado slices and fresh tomato slices are also great additions.

PORTOBELLO MARINADE

1 Tbsp. kosher salt

2 Tbsp. garlic, minced

3 Tbsp. dried basil

2 Tbsp. dried thyme

2 Tbsp. dried oregano

3 Tbsp. Dijon mustard

1 cup slow-roasted tomatoes in olive oil, (found in gourmet food section of grocery store)

½ cup red wine vinegar

½ cup rice vinegar

1 cup canola oil

2 cups virgin olive oil

Combine all ingredients except olive oil in food processor. Blend for 2 minutes, while slowly adding virgin olive oil.

CAROL'S CONCOCTION

HEIDI'S PANCAKE HOUSE • SOUTH LAKE TAHOE, CALIFORNIA

Carol's Concoction was named after one of Heidi's Pancake House's regular customers. Carol created the assembly of these ingredients, and it has remained the top-selling omelette for more than 30 years.

2 Tbsp. bacon, cooked and chopped

2 Tbsp. mushrooms, sautéed

¼ avocado, thinly sliced

⅓ – ½ cup jack cheese, grated

4 eggs, whisked

1 – 2 oz. oil

SERVES 1–2

EASIEST

Heat 8" omelette pan with oil for 30 seconds. Add eggs in pan on medium high heat. Eggs should sizzle slightly when they hit the pan. Cook eggs until bubbling-up in middle. Rotate pan to distribute eggs. Add inside ingredients except cheese. Spread ingredients evenly, not a mass in the middle of the omelette. Flip omelette with a quick flip of the wrist. Top of omelette should not be brown. Add half of the cheese. Cook another 30 - 60 seconds on low heat.

Tip pan to allow omelette to begin sliding out of the pan to the middle of the plate. Fold omelette onto plate. Top with remaining cheese.

SERVING SUGGESTION:
Serve with home fries and fresh fruit.

MOREL MUSHROOM & PANCETTA FRITTATA

RUPERT'S AT HOTEL MCCALL • CHEF GARY KUCY • MCCALL, IDAHO

Chef Kucy has been recognized by the James Beard Foundation as a semifinalist for Best Chef of the Northwest. Gary Kucy is fast establishing himself as a notable and rising star in the culinary world. In this frittata, Chef Kucy takes advantage of a favorite seasonal and local ingredient in McCall, Idaho - morel mushrooms. Morel season happens in early summer each year and foraging is a favorite pastime among locals.

1 Tbsp. butter

¼ cup morel mushrooms, sliced

5 slices pancetta

1 Tbsp. mixture parsley and thyme, freshly chopped

6 large eggs

2 Tbsp. cream

Salt and pepper to taste

3 oz. goat cheese

S ERVES **2**

Preheat oven to 350 degrees. In a medium size non-stick, oven-safe pan, melt butter and sauté pancetta and mushrooms for 3 - 4 minutes until pancetta begins to crisp. In a medium bowl, whisk eggs, cream, salt, pepper and herbs together then pour over mushroom and pancetta mixture. Reduce heat to medium-low and continue to cook until eggs begin to set. Place in oven for 12 minutes or until eggs are set and top begins to brown. Sprinkle top with cheese.

SERVING SUGGESTION:
This frittata may be served hot or cold.

CHICKEN & SUN-DRIED TOMATO QUICHE

SKI TOWN LIFE • JEN BAKER • CRESTED BUTTE, COLORADO

Jen Baker, Ski Town Life's Experiential Epicurean affectionately terms her time spent preparing meals for her family and friends as "Zen Jen Time". Recognizing that the kitchen isn't a Zen place for all people, Jen shares her tips and tricks for how to prepare easy meals at SkiTownLife.com.

4 onions, sliced and caramelized in olive oil

1 chicken breast, roasted and shredded

6 oz. jar marinated artichoke hearts, drained

⅓ cup sun-dried tomatoes

6 large eggs

1 cup heavy cream

1 tsp. garlic powder

1 tsp. salt

½ tsp. ground pepper

1 cup sharp cheddar cheese, shredded

9" pie crust, unbaked, store bought or find Jen Baker's recipe on SkiTownLife.com

Scallions, sliced

S ERVES 6 - 8

SERVING SUGGESTION:
Garnish a generous piece with additional sliced scallions.

EASIEST Preheat oven to 350 degrees. On top of unbaked crust, layer caramelized onions, shredded chicken, artichoke hearts and sun-dried tomatoes. In a large bowl, whisk together eggs, cream, garlic powder, salt and pepper. Stir in cheese. Pour egg mixture over layered ingredients. Sprinkle with sliced scallions. Bake for 60 – 75 minutes until quiche is golden and set in the center when pan is gently pushed. If crust browns too quickly, cover with foil.

THE BUNNERY'S QUICHE CRUST

THE BUNNERY BAKERY AND RESTAURANT • JACKSON, WYOMING

The Bunnery shares their Quiche Crust recipe from their acclaimed and varied offerings of quiches. Whether made with Lorraine fillings (bacon and Swiss cheese), Florentine fillings (spinach, onion and Swiss cheese) or Provencal fillings (tomato, onion, and Swiss cheese), this Quiche Crust is surely a flaky and delightful base!

2 cups all purpose flour

½ cup butter, chilled

2 Tbsp. shortening, chilled

¾ tsp. salt

⅔ tsp. sugar

4 Tbsp. ice water

MAKES 2 CRUSTS

MORE DIFFICULT

Combine dry ingredients in a bowl. Cut in chilled butter and shortening until mixture resembles small peas. One Tbsp. at a time, sprinkle ice water over crust mixture, gently gathering pastry together until combined. Divide into halves and reserve half for another quiche or freeze for up to a month. Roll one half into an 11—12" round diameter, large enough to line a 8" pie pan or tart mold. When placed in desired dish, remove excess bits and crimp the pastry around the circumference. Bake crust until slightly browned at 375 degrees, about 7 - 10 minutes.

SERVING SUGGESTION:
Fill the baked crust with desired filling and bake according to chosen quiche recipe.

HUEVOS RANCHEROS

HARDY FOARD CATERING AND THE PORCH CAFÉ • CHEF GRETCHEN HARDY •
BRATTLEBORO, VERMONT

*A go-to, hearty breakfast, Huevos Rancheros can morph into any customization. Pictured is how Chef Gretchen serves it:
over easy egg, black beans, ranchero sauce, cilantro lime crema and avocado.*

1 large onion, diced and caramelized

1 ½ cups sharp cheddar cheese, grated

3 Tbsp. parsley, freshly chopped

2 tsp. rosemary, freshly chopped

2 tsp. thyme, freshly chopped

1 tsp. sage, freshly chopped

4 cups Corn Bread, cut into 1-inch cubes, see
recipe

7 eggs

3 ½ cups heavy cream

Salt and pepper to taste

SERVES 8

MORE
DIFFICULT

Sprinkle onion, cheese, herbs and cornbread into a
buttered 9 x 11" pan. Whisk eggs with heavy cream, salt
and pepper. Pour eggs over cornbread mixture and let sit
for 10 minutes. Bake at 350 degrees for 45 minutes until
set. This can be prepared the night before and warmed in the morning.

SERVING SUGGESTION:
Serve with scallions, sour cream, Black
Beans, Cilantro Lime Crema, Ranchero
Sauce (see recipes) and salsa all on the side.

CORN BREAD

⅔ cup butter, melted

¾ cup sugar

3 eggs

1 ⅔ cups milk

2 ⅓ cups flour

1 cup corn meal

4 ½ tsp. baking powder

1 tsp. salt

Preheat oven to 400 degrees. Grease
9 x 9" pan. Mix butter, sugar and
eggs in a large bowl.

Add remaining ingredients, mix well
and pour into prepared pan. Bake for
22 - 25 minutes. This can be made
beforehand.

BLACK BEANS

2 - 15.5 oz. cans black beans,
rinsed and drained

1 tsp. cumin

1 tsp. Cajun seasoning

1 tsp. chili powder

1 small onion, small diced

2 cloves garlic, minced

½ cup orange juice

½ cup water

Salt and pepper to taste

Mix all ingredients in a large pot and
cook for 45 minutes or until onions
are soft and translucent, season with
salt and pepper. This can be made up
to 2 days in advance.

CILANTRO LIME CREMA

1 cup sour cream

2 Tbsp. cilantro, chopped

1 tsp. cumin

1 Tbsp. lime juice

Salt and pepper to taste

Mix all together in a small bowl. This can be made up to 2 days in advance.

RANCHERO SAUCE

1 medium onion, chopped

2 dried ancho chilies, soaked in hot water until soft then remove seeds and stems

1 jalapeno pepper, diced

3 cloves garlic, minced

1 cup chicken stock

2 cans diced tomatoes, fire-roasted is recommended

2 tsp. cumin

2 tsp. chili powder

1 tsp. dried oregano

1 lime, juiced

1 tsp. paprika

2 tsp. cilantro, chopped

1 Tbsp. vegetable oil

Salt and pepper to taste

Sauté peppers and onions in oil in a large saute pan until light brown. Lightly season with salt and pepper, add garlic and continue cooking for 1 – 2 minutes. Add remaining ingredients and cook for 40 minutes on low. Puree with an immersion blender until smooth. This sauce can be used cold or hot.

UP THE CREEK TOAST

SMELL THAT BREAD • STEAMBOAT SPRINGS, COLORADO

Smell That Bread specializes in rustic and artisan breads, the types of breads that conjure romantic, old-world images of wood-fired ovens and dough mixed by hand. This recipe, that uses a favorite Sourdough Rye bread from Smell That Bread, just keeps on giving. Keep any extra Whipped Chevre or Quick Pickled Onions to use as desired. They are both amazing on so many things: sandwiches, charcuterie boards, atop flatbread, etc.

Sourdough Rye loaf, ideally from Smell That Bread Bakery and sliced

2 oz. hard smoked salmon (honey smoked is recommended), shredded

2 oz. chevre cheese

1 medium red onion, thinly sliced

2 cornichons, thinly sliced

1 ½ cups rice wine vinegar

3 Tbsp. heavy cream

Black pepper

S ERVES 2

EASIEST

For the Whipped Chevre, mix chevre and cream using a paddle attachment until light and fluffy, starting on low and increasing to medium. Once chevre and cream are incorporated and it looks light and fluffy, stop mixer and scrape down sides of the bowl. Add black pepper and mix on low.

For Quick Pickled Onions, add onions in a bowl with enough rice wine vinegar to cover onions. Add black pepper and stir. Keep onions in liquid until ready to use. This is a quick pickle, so these onions can be used immediately. However, the longer they sit the better. If time allows, prepare onions the night before and let soak in refrigerator until ready to use.

Toast two slices of rye bread. Spread a thin layer of the Whipped Chevre on each slice. Top with smoked salmon. Finally, add Quick Pickled Onions and cornichons atop salmon.

SERVING SUGGESTION:
Enjoy this perfectly assembled slice of toast!

PHINEAS SWANN
EASY BLENDER EGGS BENEDICT

PHINEAS SWANN BED & BREAKFAST • CHEF DARREN DREVIK • MONTGOMERY CENTER, VERMONT

Eggs Benedict can be a daunting breakfast dish, especially with home-making hollandaise sauce. Darren and Lynne, co-owners of the Phineas Swann Bed & Breakfast don't want anyone to settle for dried, packaged hollandaise sauce. Upon experimenting, they created an easy-to-make hollandaise sauce recipe.

4 slices Canadian bacon

2 English muffins

4 egg yolks

1 Tbsp. lemon juice

8 drops Tabasco sauce

¼ tsp. salt

10 Tbsp. clarified butter

4 eggs, poached

Parsley or chives, for garnish

SERVES 2

SERVING SUGGESTION:
Garnish with fresh parsley or chives.

EASIEST Clarify butter by cooking butter over medium heat and skimming fat off surface repeatedly. When all the fat has been skimmed off the surface, the clarified butter is done.

In sauté pan, brown Canadian bacon. Toast English muffins. Poach eggs either on the stovetop or in microwave. Microwaving eggs can be an easy way to poach: crack an egg into a microwave-safe cup or bowl. Make sure the yolk stays intact. Add ⅓ cup water and 1 tsp. white vinegar, cover and microwave on 80% power for 60 – 80 seconds. Remove the egg with a slotted spoon.

For the hollandaise sauce: place egg yolks, lemon juice, Tabasco sauce and salt in a blender. Whip at highest setting for 30 seconds. Reduce blender speed to the lowest setting and add clarified butter one tablespoon at a time. Stop blending after all butter is added.

Place Canadian bacon atop opened English muffins. Add a poached egg to each and then drizzle hollandaise sauce over the top.

VEGETATION NATION

COSMOS BISTRO • CHEF CINNAMON BERG • BELLINGHAM, WASHINGTON

A popular brunch dish at Cosmos, this showcases the bounty of vegetables from local farms. Chef and owner Cinnamon Berg calls this a "breakfast salad" because the vegetables are quickly seared to stay crisp and fresh while the potatoes are roasted separately to keep the flavors from getting muddied. The herbs and cheese elevate the flavor profile of the Vegetation Nation.

1 medium sweet onion, julienned

1 bunch kale, (Lacinato recommended)

1 bunch red or rainbow chard

1 bunch arugula, cut to 2 - 3" pieces

1 lb. mushrooms, sliced (shitake, button, pioppino and oyster recommended)

2 red, yellow, purple or orange peppers, julienned

2 Tbsp. shallot, minced

1 Tbsp. garlic, minced

½ tsp. each kosher salt and black pepper

¼ cup olive oil or avocado oil

Roasted Potatoes, see recipe

Herbed Chevre, see recipe

1 Tbsp. each fresh dill, tarragon and basil, minced for garnish

SERVES 8

SERVING SUGGESTION:
Plate individual servings and top with Herbed Chevre, eggs any style and fresh herb salad.

MORE DIFFICULT

Wash all vegetables thoroughly. Remove stems of chard and kale, reserve chard stems and small dice. Cut chard and kale leaves into ½ x 2" pieces. Heat large cast iron skillet or griddle with 2 Tbsp. oil over medium high heat. Sear mushrooms and onions until starting to soften and brown, 5 - 6 minutes. Add chard stems, peppers, shallot and garlic. Add oil as needed. Toss continuously to heat through but not soften too much or burn the garlic, 3 - 4 minutes. Add Roasted Potatoes and prepped chard, kale, arugula and salt and pepper to taste. Lightly wilt the greens, cooking another 3 - 4 minutes. Top with Herbed Chevre.

ROASTED POTATOES

2 medium russet potatoes, unpeeled and diced into ½" cubes

1 large sweet potato, peeled and diced into ½" cubes

5 large red potatoes, unpeeled and diced into ½" cubes

¼ cup olive oil or avocado oil

2 – 3 Tbsp. Spice Blend, see recipe

Toss potatoes with olive oil and Spice Blend. Place on parchment lined sheet pan and roast at 425 degrees for 15 - 20 minutes.

SPICE BLEND

2 Tbsp. each Hungarian paprika, smoked paprika, granulated garlic, and black pepper

1 Tbsp. each Mexican oregano and ground coriander

1 tsp. each cumin and cayenne pepper or ground chipotle pepper

4 Tbsp. kosher salt

Mix all ingredients together.

HERBED CHEVRE

8 oz. goat cheese

1 Tbsp. each tarragon, dill and basil, minced

¼ tsp. kosher salt

¼ tsp. black pepper

2 - 3 Tbsp. half and half

Blend all ingredients and set aside.

BREAKFAST PIZZA

FULL BELLY DELI • CHEF TOM MARRIN • TRUCKEE, CALIFORNIA

According to Chef Tom, "when you're eating with a fork, all you do is push your food around the plate, looking for that perfect bite. We aim to put it on bread and give you twenty perfect bites. That's our motivation." Co-owners Eric Barton and Tom Marrin have a "we are family" mentality that exists at the deli and in the Truckee/Tahoe community. It's not rare to see the crew throwing down for charities and organizations.

1 package naan or pita bread, (Stonefire Original Naan recommended)

5 large eggs

2 cups mozzarella or provolone cheese, shredded

8 slices applewood smoked bacon

1 cup ricotta cheese

1 cup Marinara Sauce, see recipe

½ cup scallions, chopped

1 Tbsp. butter

Kosher salt

Fresh ground black pepper

S ERVES 4

SERVING SUGGESTION:
Cut pizza around the yolk into 9 small pieces, similar to a hashtag symbol.

MORE DIFFICULT

Cook bacon on sheet pan in oven at 350 degrees for 15 - 20 minutes until lightly crispy.

Chop bacon and set aside. Whip ricotta and one egg in a bowl, add a pinch each of salt and pepper then set aside. Toast naan on oven rack at 350 degrees for 3 - 5 minutes. Cook 4 sunny side up eggs by heating butter in a large nonstick skillet over low heat, until butter is melted. Crack eggs carefully into skillet and cover with a tight lid. Cook until whites are completely set but yolks are still runny, 2 – 2 ½ minutes. Season with salt and pepper.

To build pizza, spread ricotta on each piece of naan and add thin layer of Marinara Sauce. Sprinkle half of shredded cheese over marinara and gently lay a sunny side egg on top. Add chopped bacon evenly to each pizza and top with remaining cheese and salt and pepper to taste. Return to oven, low broil and cook until cheese is melted. Do not overcook yolk.

Scatter with chopped scallions.

MARINARA SAUCE

1 tsp. olive oil

1 cup yellow onion, chopped

2 cloves garlic, minced

½ cup good red wine

28-oz. can crushed tomatoes in puree, chopped

1 tsp. fresh flat-leaf parsley, chopped

Kosher salt and freshly ground black pepper to taste

Heat olive oil in large skillet. Add onions and sauté over medium heat until translucent, 5 - 10 minutes. Add garlic and cook for 1 minute. Add wine and cook on high heat, scraping brown bits, until almost all liquid evaporates, about 3 minutes. Stir in tomatoes, parsley, salt and pepper. Cover and simmer on lowest heat for 15 minutes. Blend in blender or with an immersion blender. This can be made up to 3 days ahead of time.

THE EMILY

THE WARREN STORE • WARREN, VERMONT

"Our valley is not without its characters – that's why we live here! 'Exciting Emily' has to be near the top of the list. Her enthusiasm, storytelling and zest for life are boundless. She came up with a breakfast sandwich that matched her personality, and we love it – The Emily!" states The Warren Store.

1 English muffin, well toasted

¼ cup fresh spinach, sautéed

2 tomato slices, grilled

2 slices red onion, thinly sliced

1 Boars Head sausage patty, cooked

Garlic herb boursin

1 fried egg

SERVES 1

SERVING SUGGESTION:
Enjoy with a zest for life like "Exciting Emily" has!

EASIEST

Slather boursin on both English muffin halves. Place spinach, tomato, red onion, sausage patty, and fried egg betwixt English muffin.

SALMON LOX-DILL FRITTATA

DEVIL'S THUMB RANCH • WINTER PARK, COLORADO

From Star Parties to Dinners on the Divide, Devil's Thumb Ranch offers an authentic Colorado ranch experience like no other.

1 Tbsp. butter

1 cup mozzarella, shredded

6 cups eggs

1 lb. cream cheese

4 Tbsp. fresh dill

6 oz. smoked salmon (lox)

4 Tbsp. heavy cream

SERVES 8

Preheat oven to 375 degrees. Grease a 12" cast iron pan with butter. Sprinkle mozzarella cheese on bottom of pan, layer lox and squares of cream cheese on top of mozzarella. Add fresh dill atop salmon and cream cheese. In a separate bowl, mix eggs and heavy cream until well blended. Slowly pour egg mixture over pan. Bake for 52 – 60 minutes or until set. Rest for 10 minutes before serving.

SERVING SUGGESTION:
Serve this gluten-free and keto-approved breakfast pie with a bacon-infused Bloody Mary.

CROQUE MONSIEUR OR MADAME

THE VERMILLION ROOM AT FAIRMONT BANFF SPRINGS • CHEF DE CUISINE ALEXANDRE LAFLEUR • BANFF, ALBERTA, CANADA

The Vermillion room is renowned for their weekend brunch as being the best brunch buffet in the Bow Valley. Canadian favorites and French-inspired classics are served in the newest French brasserie.

1 loaf brioche

4 whole farm eggs*

1 lb. smoked ham, sliced

¾ - 1 cup Béchamel, see recipe

½ lb. Gruyere cheese, shredded

1 Tbsp. oil or vegetable spray

S E R V E S 4

* The difference between a Croque Monsieur and Croque Madame is that the former does not have an egg in the sandwich and the latter does. This egg can be poached or fried, as in this recipe. In a pan add oil or vegetable spray and fry egg.

MORE DIFFICULT

Slice 8 pieces of brioche ¾" thick.

Spread cooled Béchamel liberally on 4 slices of brioche. Divide and layer ham onto each slice. Sprinkle cheese over all (8) slices of brioche and toast on a tray at 400 degrees for 4 minutes until golden. Assemble cheese toast and ham toast to create a Croque Monsieur or add the fried egg to make it a Croque Madame.

BÉCHAMEL

1 ¼ cups milk

¼ cup all purpose flour

¼ cup unsalted butter

⅛ tsp. ground nutmeg

Salt to taste

1 small yellow onion, peeled

In a small pot, heat on medium-low the milk and whole onion. In a separate small pan, melt butter until bubbling then add flour. Cook until it starts to smell like hazelnuts. Remove onion from milk. Slowly whisk milk into roux. Add shaved nutmeg. Add salt to taste. Remove from heat and cool in refrigerator.

SERVING SUGGESTION:
Serve aside a fresh herb salad for some brightness.

SONNENALP BAVARIAN EGGS BENEDICT

LUDWIG'S AT SONNENALP HOTEL • VAIL, COLORADO

In the heart of Vail Village, The Sonnenalp Hotel harkens back to yesteryears and an old-Bavarian style. Ludwig's is a beautifully sunlit dining room that creates the most spectacular Sunday Brunch Buffet and plated dishes that Vail has to offer.

1 tsp. table salt plus more to taste

2 Tbsp. white vinegar

4 large eggs, each cracked into a small handled cup

Ground black pepper

German rye or heavy dark bread, sliced

Black Forest ham, sliced

Hollandaise Sauce, see recipe

Fresh dill, for garnish

SERVES **2**

MORE DIFFICULT

Fill an 8 to 10-inch nonstick skillet nearly to rim with water, add 1 tsp. salt and vinegar, boil over high heat. Lower lips of each cup into water to tip eggs into boiling water, cover and remove from heat. Poach until yolks are medium-firm, 4 minutes. For firmer yolks or extra-large/jumbo eggs, poach 4 ½ minutes. For looser yolks or medium eggs, poach 3 minutes. Lift and drain each egg. Season with salt and pepper to taste.

Toast bread to liking. Pan sear Black Forest ham over medium-high heat, 2 minutes per side. Place toast on a dish, then add cooked ham and poached egg. Ladle a generous portion of Hollandaise Sauce over the eggs.

SERVING SUGGESTION:
Garnish with fresh dill.

HOLLANDAISE SAUCE

12 Tbsp. unsalted butter, softened

6 large egg yolks

½ cup boiling water

2 tsp. lemon juice

⅛ tsp. cayenne pepper

1 tsp. tomato paste

Salt

Whisk butter and egg yolks together in large heat-resistant bowl set over medium saucepan with ½ inch of barely simmering water until mixture is smooth and homogeneous. Slowly add ½ cup boiling water and cook, whisking constantly, until thickened, 7 - 10 minutes. Off heat, stir in lemon juice, tomato paste and cayenne. Season with salt to taste.

HUEVOS RANCHEROS

AFTON HOUSE INN AND CURRENT RESTAURANT • CHEF GREG MASILKO • AFTON, MINNESOTA

A recently purchased Vail Resorts 'urban resort,' Afton Alps is nestled in the scenic St. Croix River Valley just outside Minneapolis and St. Paul, Minnesota. With the Epic Pass, Midwesterners can enjoy skiing in Minnesota and take their passion to Vail Resorts' iconic western mountains. Afton Alps is truly the place where Epic begins.

2 corn tortillas

¼ cup black beans

2 eggs

⅓ cup Green Chili, see recipe

½ avocado, sliced

5 grape tomatoes, halved

1 sprig cilantro

SERVES 1

SERVING SUGGESTION:
The Green Chili is a meal within itself, so reserve leftovers for lunch another day.

MORE DIFFICULT

Fry tortillas until crisp or just heat and leave soft. Place beans on center of plate to form a stable base for the tortillas. Place tortillas on top of beans, then top with eggs cooked to liking, top the eggs with Green Chili, avocado, tomatoes, and cilantro.

GREEN CHILI

1 lb. pork, ground

2 Tbsp. butter

3 cups pork stock or chicken stock

½ lb. Anaheim pepper, roasted, peeled, and diced

½ lb. Poblano pepper, roasted, peeled, and diced

2 lbs. tomatillo, husked and grilled

⅓ cup masa

½ cup cilantro, minced

½ cup green onion, roughly cut

1 tsp. crushed red pepper

2 tsp. salt

1 tsp. black pepper

½ tsp. cumin

2 Tbsp. lime juice

Olive oil

Lightly oil and grill peppers until skin blisters turning to make sure skin blisters evenly. After roasting, place in a bowl and cover with cling wrap to trap the heat and allow to cool. The skin will separate from the peppers making them easier to peel. Remove skin and seeds from peppers under cool running water then dice to ¼". Peel, halve, and grill tomatillos. Process tomatillos, green onions, cilantro and lime juice in a blender or food processor until smooth. In a large pot, brown pork in butter with salt, pepper, red pepper and cumin. Once browned add in masa and cook on medium heat while stirring for five minutes to cook the masa into the pork mixture, add tomatillo mixture and diced peppers and bring to a simmer. The longer this simmers the more the flavors will develop.

WALDHAUS SMOKED ROCKY MOUNTAIN TROUT BENEDICT

**WALDHAUS RESTAURANT AT FAIRMONT BANFF SPRINGS • CHEF DE CUISINE SEAN FISHER •
BANFF, ALBERTA, CANADA**

*Loosen the lederhosen and head down to Banff's best kept secret, the Waldhaus! This "little house in the woods" is the
ultimate place to relax and enjoy the mountain scenery all around you. Sample a superb Bavarian beer selection and the
alpine-inspired cuisine such as Alpine frittatas, Black Forest French Toast, seasonally-inspired waffles and signature egg
benedicts, like this recipe.*

1 – 1 ¼ lbs. smoked trout filet or 16 slices thick-cut Canadian bacon

8 large farm eggs

8 Potato Rösti, see recipe

2 cups hollandaise sauce, store bought or home-make a favorite recipe*

Fresh dill or parsley

Smoked paprika

4 heirloom tomatoes, chopped

Mix of kale, baby kale, spinach and frisée lettuce

Lemon Pepper Vinaigrette, see recipe

1 Tbsp. white wine vinegar

2 – 3 Tbsp. olive oil

Fresh herbs, for garnish

S E R V E S   4

MOST DIFFICULT

In a medium pot filled with water, add vinegar and simmer. In a 350 degree oven, roast local heirloom tomatoes with olive oil and salt for 10 minutes. Keep warm. Flake hot smoked trout filet into bite-sized pieces and warm in oven or gently in a frying pan. If Canadian bacon is chosen, pan fry in a large cast iron pan. Keep warm. In a mixing bowl combine lettuces with Lemon Pepper Vinaigrette. In simmering pot of water and vinegar, crack eggs and poach for 2 ½ - 3 minutes. Remove eggs and drain on a clean kitchen cloth or paper towel.

On plates, place two Potato Rösti each and garnish with smoked trout flakes or Canadian bacon. Add poached eggs on top and garnish the plates with roasted heirloom tomatoes and greens tossed with the vinaigrette. Add a generous amount of hollandaise sauce (*If you'd like to peruse Chef de Cuisine Sean Fisher's Hollandaise Sauce recipe, see www.skitownlife.com).

SERVING SUGGESTION:
If trout was chosen, garnish with paprika and fresh dill sprigs. If Canadian bacon was chosen, garnish with fresh parsley and pea tendrils.

POTATO RÖSTI

4 large Yukon gold potatoes

½ cup red onion, finely diced

½ cup capers, chopped

⅛ cup fresh dill, finely chopped

⅛ cup Italian parsley, finely chopped

1 lemon, zested and juiced

2 egg yolks

1 Tbsp. corn starch

Salt and pepper to taste

2 Tbsp. butter

2 Tbsp. canola oil

Par-bake potatoes on a salt bed for 20 - 30 minutes at 350 degrees then cool. Grate potatoes on cheese grater into large bowl. Add remaining ingredients except butter and canola oil. Scoop ½ cup portions and press into round shapes on parchment paper. In a large cast iron pan, heat butter and canola oil over medium-high heat, sear the potato rösti until golden brown. Finish cooking the rösti in a 350 degree oven for 6 - 8 minutes. Drain on paper towel.

LEMON PEPPER VINAIGRETTE

½ cup olive oil

⅛ cup lemon juice, freshly squeezed

2 Tbsp. pure maple syrup

1 tsp. black pepper, freshly cracked

Salt to taste

In a mixing bowl, combine all ingredients to create vinaigrette. Adjust the acidity or sweetness to taste by adding lemon juice and maple syrup.

BAKED EGG SCRAMBLE

BRODER ØST • HOOD RIVER, OREGON

Broder Øst, serving Portland's premier Nordic brunch, finds its home in the Historic Hood River Hotel, which is on the National Register of Historic Places. The bounty of the gorge is highlighted in traditional and lovingly crafted Scandinavian dishes in this European inspired hideaway.

4 eggs

2 Tbsp. heavy cream

5 cherry tomatoes

2 Tbsp. chevre

Fresh parsley, minced

Fresh chives, minced

2 Tbsp. caramelized onions

Salt and pepper to taste

Oil or butter for pan

SERVES 1 - 2

Preheat oven to 400 degrees. Bake cherry tomatoes seasoned with salt and pepper on a sheet pan until tomatoes are blistered. Caramelize onions in an oiled or buttered pan on the stovetop at medium heat for 10-15 minutes. It is better to cook the onions low and slow, as onions should be soft and brown, not crisp and burnt. Beat eggs with heavy cream. In a separate bowl, whip together chevre cheese and herbs. Add all ingredients evenly spread in a cast iron skillet then pour in egg mixture and bake at 400 degrees, for about 10-15 minutes or until set.

SERVING SUGGESTION:
Serve with a toasted slice of walnut bread and butter.

SAUSAGE ROLLS

BIG EYES BAKERY • BAKER BRIGID FAENZA • LUDLOW, VERMONT

After retiring from the NYPD, baker Brigid Faenza received a masters in baking from the New School in NYC and started a home-based bakery business selling baked goods at farmer's markets in Peekskill, New York and other areas. In 2014 Brigid opened Big Eyes Bakery in Ludlow, Vermont, but not before traveling to Ireland where Brigid observed many roadside shops selling Sausage Rolls around the countryside.

1 lb. store-bought puff pastry

1 lb. bulk sweet Italian sausage meat

¼ cup Italian bread crumbs

¼ cup onion, minced

2 tsp. garlic, minced

½ tsp. black pepper

1 ½ tsp. cumin

1 tsp. paprika

1 egg

1 egg yolk (reserve egg white for brushing pastry squares)

2 tsp. milk

Extra milk for brushing

SERVES **12**

Preheat oven to 350 degrees. Line a baking sheet with parchment paper. Put all ingredients in a bowl, except puff pastry and egg white, and mix together. Roll out the pastry on a lightly floured work surface and cut into 12 squares. Brush each square with egg white. Place ¼ cup of sausage mixture on each square and roll up the pastry. Transfer to sheet pan with the seam down. Brush with milk. Bake for 20-25 minutes until golden brown.

SERVING SUGGESTION:
Enjoy these decadent rolls with a fresh herbed salad on the side.

SHRIMP & GREEN MOLE GRITS

FULL BELLY DELI • CHEF TOM MARRIN • TRUCKEE, CALIFORNIA

Green mole or "Mole Verde" is a type of Mexican mole. Mole is a sauce spiced with earthy, rich flavors. Green mole uses pumpkin seeds and chilies or pepper along with fresh greens.

1 lb. large shrimp, peeled, deveined, and tail on

1 cup stone ground grits

4 cups water or chicken stock

4 slices bacon, chopped

3 Tbsp. unsalted butter

4 eggs, poached

4 tsp. white vinegar

Kosher salt and fresh ground pepper to taste

Green Mole, see recipe

Scallions, for garnish

SERVES 4

Break each egg into a small bowl. Fill a large, straight-sided skillet or Dutch oven with 2 inches of water; bring to a boil. Add vinegar. Reduce to a gentle simmer: the water should be steaming and small bubbles should come up from the bottom of the pan. Submerging the lip of each bowl into the simmering water, gently add the eggs, one at a time.

Cook for 4 minutes for soft set, 5 minutes for medium set and 8 minutes for hard set. Using a slotted spoon, transfer the eggs to a clean dish towel to drain. If done ahead of time, reheat eggs in simmering water for 1 minute.

In a separate pot, boil 4 cups stock or water. Add salt and pepper. Add grits and cook until water is absorbed, about 20 - 25 minutes. Remove from heat and stir in butter. Set aside.

Rinse shrimp and pat dry. Fry bacon in a large skillet until browned; drain well. In bacon fat, add shrimp. Cook until shrimp turns pink. Add desired amount of Green Mole to coat shrimp thoroughly, add chopped bacon and sauté for 3 minutes. Divide grits evenly between 4 bowls; top each with a poached egg. Divide shrimp among bowls and add more Green Mole if desired.

SERVING SUGGESTION:
Garnish with chopped scallions.

GREEN MOLE

1 cup pumpkin seeds, hulled and untoasted

2 Tbsp. sesame seeds

1 tsp. cumin seeds

1 lb. tomatillos, soaked and husked

1 jalapeno pepper

1 poblano pepper

1 anaheim pepper

½ white onion, cut in half

2 garlic cloves, peeled

5 green Swiss chard leaves, stems removed and chopped

½ bunch cilantro, chopped

2 cups chicken stock

¼ cup olive oil

Salt and pepper to taste

Add tomatillos, peppers, onions and garlic to large bowl, toss with 2 Tbsp. olive oil and salt and pepper. Place mixture on sheet pan in a pile to protect garlic and onion from burning. Roast for 20 - 40 minutes in 375 degree oven.

In a dry skillet, cook cumin seeds and sesame seeds over medium heat, stirring constantly until deep golden, about 5 minutes. Spread on tray to cool. Put pumpkin seeds in pan and stir until they begin to swell and start to pop, about 3 minutes. Set aside. When cooled, grind sesame and cumin to a slightly textured powder. Then grind pumpkin seeds to same texture. Transfer both to a bowl and stir in 1 cup chicken stock to make a thick paste. Put 1 cup chicken stock into blender and add roasted tomatillos, onion, peppers, garlic and blend until fairly smooth. Gradually add half of Swiss chard and blend as smoothly as possible. Add rest of greens with just enough of the chicken stock to enable the blades of the blender to work efficiently. Add the toasted seeds and blend quickly.

Put blended mixture in large skillet and cook over medium heat, stirring frequently, until sauce reduces and thickens, for 10 minutes. Add more chicken stock if sauce is too thick. Cook for 10 more minutes. Set aside to cool and put in airtight container. Reserve in refrigerator.

FARM-RAISED FRIED EGG ATOP EVERYTHING SPICED GARLIC NAAN BREAD
with Accompaniments

THE WENTWORTH INN • CHEF BRIAN GAZDA • JACKSON, NEW HAMPSHIRE

The Wentworth is an elegant country inn amidst the majestic White Mountains of Jackson, New Hampshire. The idyllic setting provides a temporary escape from life's everyday stresses and allows guests the freedom to reconnect, rediscover, and recharge with abundant possibilities in nature.

½ cup warm water

¼ tsp. dry instant yeast

2 ¼ cups all purpose flour, sifted

1 Tbsp. sugar

1 Tbsp. salt

½ cup plain yogurt

2 tsp. Everything Spice Seasoning, see recipe

1 bunch green onions, finely chopped

1 Tbsp. garlic oil

3 Tbsp. butter, melted

6 farm-raised eggs

Tomato Chutney, see recipe

Iberico ham, Gruyere cheese and sautéed asparagus, for garnish

SERVES 6

MOST DIFFICULT

In large mixing bowl, combine warm water with yeast. Rest at room temperature until a froth develops, 10 minutes. Sift flour in deep bowl. Mix activated yeast mixture with flour until dough comes together. Add yogurt, Everything Spice Seasoning, sugar and salt; gently combine. Add green onions to mixture. Knead dough gently with hands adding garlic oil until just soft and slightly pliable. Place dough in garlic oiled bowl and cover bowl with a damp cloth. Let rest at room temperature until the dough doubles in size, about 2 hours. Separate dough into six equal portions and lightly flour; dough will be sticky. Roll each piece into an oval shape 8 x 3". Naan should be ¼" thick. Transfer each piece to hot cast iron skillet lightly coated with garlic oil and cook for 1 minute each side. Lightly brush with butter and Everything Spice Seasoning and let rest on a wire rack. Spread Tomato Chutney on a plate and lay naan bread across it. Fry a farm-raised egg sunny side up and gently place on top.

EVERYTHING SPICE SEASONING

4 Tbsp. kosher salt

2 Tbsp. white sesame seeds, roasted

2 Tbsp. black sesame seeds, roasted

2 Tbsp. caraway seeds, roasted and ground

2 Tbsp. onion powder

2 Tbsp. garlic powder

2 Tbsp. ground black pepper

Mix together all ingredients for a spice blend.

SERVING SUGGESTION:
Accompaniments can include lightly sautéed fresh asparagus, shaved Iberico ham, micro greens tossed in olive oil, salt and pepper, additional Tomato Chutney and shaved Gruyere cheese.

TOMATO CHUTNEY

1 #10 can (2 quarts) Alta Cucina plum tomatoes, drained and crushed*

4 cups white wine vinegar

2 cups sugar

1 cup shallots, chopped

1 ½ Tbsp. yellow mustard seeds

1 ½ Tbsp. allspice

¾ cup golden raisins

¼ cup currants or dried cherries

1 ½ Tbsp. fresh ground black pepper

1 ½ Tbsp. sea salt

*Save the drained liquid for use in soup recipes from *Ski Town Soups*.

Combine sugar and ½ cup of water in stainless pot and simmer over medium heat until amber in color. Add all other ingredients and cook over low heat for 1-1 ½ hours. The mixture will reduce greatly and produce about 4 cups of chutney.

HUEVOS RANCHEROS

GOLDMINER'S DAUGHTER LODGE • CHEF SAM HOLDER • ALTA, UTAH

Sam Holder is one of the executive chefs at the Goldminer's Daughter Lodge in Alta, UT. He has worked in kitchens all over the country for the last 15 years, running the gamut from fine dining to greasy-spoon diners. The seasonal life provides him with the opportunity to make delicious food in the winter and travel during the summer. Hailing from Kansas City, Chef Sam has a deep and abiding love for large chunks of meat, smoked slow-and-low, on a crisp fall day.

1 15-oz. can black beans

1 cup Homemade Salsa, plus more for plating, see recipe

4 yellow or white corn tortillas

½ cup vegetable oil

4 large eggs

1 Tbsp. butter

SERVES 4

MORE DIFFICULT

Drain and rinse black beans, cook salsa and beans in a saucepan over medium heat until hot. Heat vegetable oil in a high-sided skillet. Fry tortillas on both sides until crispy, remove from oil and place on paper towel. Heat butter in non-stick skillet over medium-low heat until just melted. Crack an egg into a small bowl and add to hot butter. Cook 4 - 6 minutes until whites are set. Assemble by laying crispy tortillas on 4 individual plates. Top with a scoop of beans then an extra scoop of Homemade Salsa. Gently lay a sunny side up egg on top.

HOMEMADE SALSA

2 cups canned tomatoes, ½ liquid drained

1 large clove garlic, chopped

1 yellow onion, large diced

¼ cup cilantro, roughly chopped

1 medium jalapeno, seeds removed

1 ½ Tbsp. lime juice

1 tsp. kosher salt

Add all ingredients to a food processor and pulse a few times until desired consistency.

SERVING SUGGESTION:
Garnish with Queso Fresco cheese and a few cilantro leaves.

BUBBLE & SQUEAK

JIMMY'S RESTAURANT AT THE LANDING RESORT AND SPA • SOUTH LAKE TAHOE, CALIFORNIA

'Bubble & Squeak' is a classic British dish made primarily from leftovers. The name comes from what is seen and heard when making it: the butter bubbles while the cabbage squeaks. Ski town residents oftentimes have many weekend visitors during ski season; this dish utilizes leftover ingredients and is chock full of vegetables, potatoes, and protein getting skiers out the door without much fuss. Traditionally made with potatoes and cabbage, Bubble & Squeak can be made with any vegetables or meats and can be prepared the night before and ready to bake in the morning.

½ cup butter, room temperature

1 ¼ cups cooked potatoes, mashed or roasted

1 cup cooked cabbage

1 cup spinach

4 Tbsp. shallot

4 cloves garlic

4 Tbsp. cooked bacon

6 Tbsp. cooked sausage

1 egg

2 Tbsp. bread crumbs

Salt and pepper to taste

8 eggs, poached, optional

Hollandaise sauce, optional

SERVES **4**

EASIEST

Add all ingredients except butter, poached egg and hollandaise sauce to a food processor. Chop and mix until fully incorporated. Heavily butter a shallow muffin tin and portion the mix evenly into 8 portions. Bake at 350 degrees for 30 - 40 minutes. They are done when tops are browned and the "Heavenly" smell permeates the kitchen. Rest in muffin tins for at least 5 minutes before removing.

SERVING SUGGESTION:
At Jimmy's Restaurant, this is served with a perfectly poached egg and drizzled with velvety hollandaise sauce.

BREAKFAST QUESADILLA

GOLDMINER'S DAUGHTER LODGE • CHEF SAM HOLDER • ALTA, UTAH

Situated at the foot of Alta Ski Area and a short shuttle from Snowbird, the Goldminer's Daughter Lodge is a home away from home while skiing the steepest and deepest Utah has to offer. The "Greatest Snow on Earth" is extremely easy to access as Goldminer's Daughter Lodge is located 45 minutes from Salt Lake International Airport.

4 large eggs, beaten

½ red onion, diced

½ green bell pepper, diced

¼ cup crimini mushrooms, diced

6 slices bacon, mostly cooked and chopped

2 Tbsp. butter

Salt and pepper to taste

1 cup Monterey jack cheese, shredded

1 12 – 14" flour tortilla

Sour cream and salsa, for garnish

SERVES 1 – 2

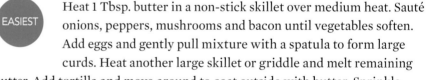

EASIEST

Heat 1 Tbsp. butter in a non-stick skillet over medium heat. Sauté onions, peppers, mushrooms and bacon until vegetables soften. Add eggs and gently pull mixture with a spatula to form large curds. Heat another large skillet or griddle and melt remaining butter. Add tortilla and move around to coat outside with butter. Sprinkle with cheese and melt. After egg filling is cooked, spread evenly over tortilla. Fold tortilla in half, remove from heat and slice into 4 triangular pieces.

SERVING SUGGESTION:
Serve with sour cream and your choice of salsa.

EGGS BENEDICT

SNOWMASS CLUB • ASPEN, COLORADO

Snowmass Club is a private member's club located 8,000 feet above sea level amid landmark mountain peaks and a short drive from Aspen. This exclusive membership offers extensive amenities, as well as the world's largest luxury exchange program. Over 240 Registry Collection properties in over 44 countries around the world can be utilized through the Reciprocity Program."

2 English muffins, toasted

4 slices Canadian bacon

4 eggs, poached

4 egg yolks

1 Tbsp. lemon juice, freshly squeezed

½ cup unsalted butter, melted

Pinch cayenne

Pinch salt

Splash white vinegar

Parsley and sautéed asparagus, for garnish

SERVES 2

 MORE DIFFICULT To make the hollandaise sauce, vigorously whisk egg yolks and lemon juice together in a stainless steel bowl until mixture is thickened and doubled in volume. Place bowl over a saucepan containing barely simmering water; the water should not touch the bottom of the bowl. Drizzle in butter and whisk until thickened. Remove from heat, whisk in cayenne and salt. Cover and reserve in a warm spot. If sauce gets too thick, whisk in a few drops of warm water.

Brown Canadian bacon in a medium skillet and toast English muffins. Fill a 10-inch nonstick skillet half full of water. Add white vinegar and slowly boil. Gently break eggs into water and simmer. Cook 3 ½ minutes until egg white is set and yolk remains soft. Remove with a slotted spoon, allowing egg to drain. Lay a slice of Canadian bacon on top of each muffin half, followed by a poached egg. Season with salt and pepper. Spoon hollandaise sauce over eggs.

SERVING SUGGESTION:
Garnish Eggs Benedict with chopped parsley and serve alongside sautéed asparagus.

EGGS ON BELLY

STOWEFLAKE MOUNTAIN RESORT & SPA • CHEF CHRISTOPH WINGENSIEFEN • STOWE, VERMONT

Originally founded in 1963, Stoweflake has grown from a modest inn into a premier 4-diamond luxury resort known as America's spa destination - voted a Top Spa by readers of Condé Nast Traveler. Stoweflake Mountain Resort is owned and operated by three generations. The Baraw family remains dedicated to each other, hospitality excellence and simple elegance.

1 English muffin, toasted

2 slices pork belly, precooked

2 eggs, poached

Hollandaise sauce, store bought or home-make a favorite recipe

BBQ sauce, store bought or home-make a favorite recipe

3 spears asparagus, blanched

¼ cup fresh tomatoes, diced

1 stalk green onion

2 tsp. vinegar

SERVES 1

Poach eggs in lightly boiling water with vinegar, about 3 – 4 minutes. Sear pork belly in a medium-hot sauté pan. Mix together hollandaise sauce and BBQ sauce in a 2:1 or 3:1 ratio. Lay toasted English muffin halves on a plate. Place warmed pork belly and poached eggs on top of muffins. Drizzle ample hollandaise and BBQ sauce mixture over the eggs.

SERVING SUGGESTION:
Garnish the plate with blanched asparagus, diced tomatoes and green onion stalk.

HIGH COUNTRY SHRIMP & GRITS
with Red-Eye Gravy

LOULA'S CAFÉ • CHEF SHAUN MCCOLLUM • WHITEFISH, MONTANA

Chef Shaun furthered his love for food by earning a honors culinary degree from Scottsdale Culinary Institute. After working at a five-diamond Scottsdale resort, he was beckoned back to Whitefish where his culinary talent blossoms and grows, contributing to Loula's ever-present success.

4 cups milk

1 cup grits

2 tsp. salt

½ tsp. pepper

1 cup sharp cheddar cheese, shredded

1 - 2 lbs. shrimp, peeled, deveined and tails-on

Red Eye Gravy, see recipe

SERVES 6

SERVING SUGGESTION:
"Bon Appetit," exclaims Chef Shaun!

MORE DIFFICULT

In a medium pot, add milk, grits, salt and pepper and heat on medium. Whisk ingredients until grits thicken. Turn off burner and add cheese. Whisk until cheese melts. Pour cheesy grits into a greased 9 x 11" pan and refrigerate. Once cooled, cut grits into squares. These can be made 2 - 3 days in advance. When ready to serve, heat a large frying pan with a little oil. Sear grit cakes on both sides until heated through. Season shrimp with salt and pepper and cook to liking: grilled, sautéed, baked, etc.

Place heated grit cakes in the middle of plates. Top with cooked shrimp and then ladle Red-Eye Gravy over the top.

RED-EYE GRAVY

½ cup butter

1 onion, small diced

1 red bell pepper, small diced

1 green bell pepper, small diced

½ yellow bell pepper, small diced

3 sausage links, chopped (any sausage: Cajun, Andouille, etc.)

2 cloves garlic, chopped

1 tsp. salt

1 tsp. pepper

½ cup flour

1 tsp. fresh thyme, chopped

1 tsp. chili powder

1 tsp. paprika

1 tsp. Worcestershire sauce

2 cups coffee

1 cup Madeira sweet wine (or another sweet wine, like sherry)

½ can V8 vegetable juice

1 ½ - 2 ½ cups chicken stock

In a medium pot over medium heat, melt butter and brown sausage. While browning, add chili powder, paprika, and thyme. Add onions, peppers, garlic, salt and pepper. Cook until onions start to soften, stirring constantly. Pour in sweet wine and reduce for 3 minutes. Add flour and stir continuously until incorporated. Pour in coffee and whisk. Once boiling and thickening, add Worcestershire sauce and V8 juice. Continue whisking and add chicken stock. Once gravy consistency is reached, place on low heat to keep warm. This can be made in advance and reheated with water or chicken stock to thin.

GENERATIONS MAIN STREET SKILLET

GENERATIONS AT GOLDEN ARROW LAKESIDE RESORT • CHEF CHRISTOPHER MCDERMOTT • LAKE PLACID, NEW YORK

Generations at Golden Arrow Lakeside Resort simply desired to offer a hash & eggs dish with a twist. It features corned beef hash, two farm fresh poached eggs and grilled asparagus topped with green onion hollandaise sauce and oven roasted tomatoes. This popular item on the Generations menu is called "Main Street Skillet" because, well, the restaurant is located on Main Street in Lake Placid.

2 farm fresh eggs, sourced from Giroux's Farm

½ can corned beef hash

6 - 8 spears asparagus

3 oz. hollandaise sauce, store bought or home-make a favorite recipe

¼ cup chives, freshly chopped

1 Roma tomato, quartered and oven roasted (sun-dried tomato also works)

¼ cup unsalted butter

SERVES 1

EASIEST

Poach two eggs in water with a splash of white vinegar on stovetop until medium. Cook corned beef hash in a individual size cast iron skillet until crispy. Pan sear asparagus spears in melted butter with a pinch of salt and pepper. Heat store-bought or homemade hollandaise sauce on low and incorporate chopped chives.

SERVING SUGGESTION:
In a single serving skillet, top hash with poached eggs and hollandaise sauce then add seared asparagus and roasted tomatoes.

MACHACA BURRITO

THE BREAKFAST CLUB • CHEF SUE EBERSOLD • MAMMOTH LAKES, CALIFORNIA

The Breakfast Club is a cow-themed, home-style, mountain-country kind of place with an old fashioned, cozy atmosphere. Opened in 1986 and serving the best grub ever since, it's known for generous portions, homemade baked goods, and Cakes By Sue!

Burrito Filling, see recipe

1 cup pico de gallo, store bought or home-make a favorite recipe

8 eggs

2 cups mixture of jack and cheddar cheese, shredded

8 flour tortillas

Salsa verde, store bought or home-make a favorite recipe

SERVES 8

Place Burrito Filling in skillet with pico de gallo and cook until hot. Add eggs and scramble together then add 1 cup cheese. Spoon mixture atop large flour tortillas set on oven-safe plates. Cover with salsa verde and remaining cheese then melt cheese on top under a broiler.

BURRITO FILLING

2 ½ - 3 lbs. chuck roast, cubed

2 tomatoes, sliced

1 large onion, peeled and chopped

1 large green bell pepper, chopped

2 jalapenos, halved

½ cup beef broth per lb. of meat

½ tsp. garlic powder

½ tsp. cumin

1 tsp. paprika

1 tsp. black pepper

2 tsp. chili powder

½ tsp. salt

1 – 14 oz. can tomato sauce

Add all ingredients in a Dutch oven or large soup pot. Cook covered on low heat for 2 ½ hours then uncovered for 1 hour. Remove and shred cooked beef. Puree remaining pot of ingredients with an immersion blender.

SERVING SUGGESTION:

Serve with home fries, which can be sliced red potatoes sautéed with chopped red and green bell peppers and diced onions.

PORK BELLY & EGG BRUNCH

MOUNTAIN VIEW GRAND RESORT • WHITEFIELD, NEW HAMPSHIRE

U.S. News & World Report ranks the best hotels by taking into account reputation among professional travel experts, guest reviews and hotel class ratings. In 2017, Mountain View Grand received #1 on the "Best Hotels of New Hampshire' list.

8 oz. raw pork belly

¼ cup mire poix*, roughly chopped

4 garlic cloves

3 cups ham stock

1 cup apple cider

Tomato Conserve, see recipe

Hollandaise Sauce, see recipe

1 cup fresh spinach

2 oz. pickle juice

Salt to taste

2 eggs

2 slices sourdough bread

Splash distilled vinegar

*Mire poix is equal parts carrots, onions and celery.

SERVES 1

MOST DIFFICULT

Salt and sear pork belly on both sides. Place in a baking dish with mire poix* and garlic. Cover pork belly with ham stock and apple cider. Cover baking dish with aluminum foil. Cook in a 350 degree oven for 4 hours. When cooked, cool in liquid. Remove pork belly and place on sheet tray. Place another tray on top and compress pork belly with something heavy. Refrigerate overnight. Cut pork into 1 ½ x 1 ½" cubes. Lightly fry pork.

Over medium-high heat, sauté spinach, pickle juice and 2 Tbsp. water until cooked through. Season with salt. Lightly boil water and vinegar in a saucepot. Crack eggs gently into the water and cook until whites solidify. Cut the crusts off the bread and cut into 2 triangles, toast to desired darkness.

Alternate toast points with warm pork belly cubes on a plate, spoon Tomato Conserve on top of pork, then place spinach on opposite sides of toast points. Place poached eggs on top of toast points and pour Hollandaise Sauce on top of eggs.

TOMATO CONSERVE

3 cups fresh tomatoes, blanched and peeled

2 cups granulated sugar

1 cinnamon stick

4 cloves

1 lemon, ¼" diced

½ Tbsp. orange, ¼" diced

Combine all ingredients in saucepot. Cook on medium-low heat until most liquid is evaporated and mixture thickens. Remove cinnamon stick and cool.

HOLLANDAISE SAUCE

2 egg yolks

1 quart clarified butter, melted

½ cup lemon juice

Salt to taste

Tabasco sauce

Whisk egg yolks and lemon juice over double boiler until thick and frothy. Remove from heat; slowly whisk in melted butter. If sauce looks like it is about to separate, whisk in a small amount of cold water. When it comes together continue adding butter. Season with salt and Tabasco sauce to taste.

SERVING SUGGESTION:
For a dash of color, distribute a pinch of paprika around the plate.

BREAKFAST PANINI

HOLY GRILL • CALGARY, ALBERTA, CANADA

Both Holy Grill locations are based in Calgary, which is a bit farther from Fernie but worth the visit. If weekend-warrior-ing, grab a bite before heading to Fernie Alpine Resort for a ski weekend. Breakfast is served all day on Saturday and Sunday at Holy Grill's 10th Avenue location, so you know it's not to be missed!

12-inch pita or flat bread

2 Tbsp. togarashi mayo, or hot sauce mixed with mayonnaise

4 slices white cheddar

1 tsp. green onions, chopped

4 strips bacon, cooked crispy

1 Tbsp. jalapeños, pickled

3 eggs

2 cups spinach

1 tomato, thickly sliced

1 pickle

Salt and pepper to taste

Random piece of fruit

Random baked good, like a donut

SERVES 1

In a large pan, cook eggs until over medium. Remove and rest. Sauté spinach seasoned with salt and pepper to taste. Spread surface of pita bread with togarashi mayo. On the center of the pita, add cheddar in stacks of two side-by-side then add bacon, green onions, pickled jalapeños, and cooked eggs. Finish by adding sautéed spinach and sliced tomatoes. Salt and pepper tomatoes to taste.

Fold sides of pita like wrapping a burrito. Cooked wrapped panini in a pan on both sides until golden brown. Use another frying pan to press down while panini is cooking. Cut panini diagonally.

SERVING SUGGESTION:

Assemble a 6-inch skewer through a pickle, a baked good, and a fresh piece of fruit, like a gooseberry then pierce the skewer through the Breakfast Panini.

MONTANA "DENVER" OMELETTE

THE LODGE AT WHITEFISH LAKE • CHEF THOMAS NEWTON • WHITEFISH, MONTANA

The Lodge at Whitefish Lake has returned a sense of leisure and grace to the Montana travel experience. Surrounded by mountains with the pristine waters of Whitefish Lake at its back door, and all the amenities of a full-service resort hotel, The Lodge at Whitefish Lake is reminiscent of grand lodges of the past with all the conveniences of the present.

12 eggs

4 Tbsp. butter

2 Tbsp. olive oil

¼ cup yellow onion, finely diced

¼ cup green pepper, finely diced

1 lb. ground elk

1 Tbsp. kosher salt

1 tsp. ground white pepper

½ Tbsp. granulated garlic

½ Tbsp. onion powder

1 tsp. ground cumin

½ tsp. dark chili powder

1 cup cheddar jack cheese, shredded

Cilantro Crema, see recipe

SERVES 4

Season ground elk by mixing salt, white pepper, granulated garlic, onion powder, cumin, and chili powder together and seasoning the ground elk. Heat large skillet on medium-high heat with olive oil. Add yellow onions and cook 2 - 4 minutes until onions soften. Add green peppers and seasoned ground elk and cook, stirring frequently, for 4 - 6 minutes until ground elk is cooked. Drain oil and fat from pan and set aside, keeping covered and warm.

Crack eggs in medium sized bowls, 3 eggs per omelette and whisk thoroughly. Heat 10-inch nonstick pan with 1 Tbsp. butter on medium-high heat, swirling pan to cover bottom with butter. Add eggs, gently work with a spatula to lift the edges of eggs as cooking (this allows uncooked egg to move underneath). Once eggs are mostly cooked with very little liquid on top, flip and cook topside down for 1 minute. While top of omelette is facedown spread ¼ cup of shredded cheese across omelette and melt. Slide omelette onto plate, add ¼ of the cooked elk mixture on top of the cheese and roll the egg into an omelette like a burrito. Continue with other 3 omelettes. Drizzle generously with Cilantro Crema.

SERVING SUGGESTION:
Serve with hash browns and Wheat Montana Sourdough toast.

CILANTRO CREMA

2 cups sour cream

¼ cup cilantro, chopped

1 tsp. kosher salt

1 tsp. lemon juice

¼ cup heavy cream (or milk)

Mix sour cream, cilantro, salt, lemon juice, and cream thoroughly in a food processor, blender or by hand. It tends to be thinner and drizzle easier when blended by machine.

SMOKED DUCK GNOCCHI

FLANNEL AT TOPNOTCH RESORT • STOWE, VERMONT

Flannel is a place that pays homage to Vermont fresh ingredients, seasonal inspirations, world-class wines, and service – paced to please. At Flannel, the pleasure of eating befits the joy of dining. Because when guests gather, amidst magical views of the mountains, an imaginative dining experience ensues. Elicited by the relaxed coziness of being at the table and heightened by what's on the menu.

1 lb. ricotta

1 large egg

1 - 2 cups OO flour, also called doppio zero flour used for pasta-making

1 oz. parmesan cheese, grated

1 tsp. kosher salt

1 tsp. pepper, freshly ground

Smoked Duck, see recipe

SERVES 2 – 4

MOST DIFFICULT

Mix all ingredients except Smoked Duck until dough ball forms then roll into ¼" sticks. Cut into 1" gnocchi and drop in boiling water until floating, about 3 minutes. Remove and cool.

SMOKED DUCK

Duck breast

Sugar

Salt

Apple wood chips

Pat the duck breast dry. Pack with a cure of sugar and salt in a 1:1 ratio. Cure for 1 day in the refrigerator. Remove from cure and brush off remnants. Place on top rack of roasting pan and line the bottom of roasting pan with aluminum foil. Spread apple wood chips evenly on foil. Leaving duck breast off pan, cook wood chips at 450 degrees until they start to smolder. Remove pan from oven and place duck breast on rack atop wood chip pan and tightly wrap pan with aluminum foil. Let sit for 2 hours.

Duck can be wrapped with 2 layers of cheese cloth and bound with butchers twine. This can be kept for 2 weeks in the refrigerator.

SERVING SUGGESTION:
Enjoy gnocchi recipe with any sauce or accompaniment; Topnotch Resort plates the gnocchi with smoked duck and a sunny side up egg.

STEAMBOAT SKILLET

SOMERS BAY CAFE • SOMERS, MONTANA

Somers Bay Café is a true family affair! Dennis Hatton was the mastermind of the project of restoring the original brick building, but quickly and lovingly, family members have arrived and stayed. His son, James Hatton, an honors graduate of the University of Montana, spent nearly 5 years as a combat platoon commander of the Marine Corps before his heart beckoned him home. The philosophy of the café is to research recipes for a base and adjust to their liking.

½ russet potato, chopped and boiled

1 cup sharp cheddar cheese, shredded

2 slices bacon, cooked and crumbled

¼ cup sausage, cooked and crumbled

¼ cup ham, cooked and chopped

2 Tbsp. tomato, diced

2 Tbsp. onion, chopped and sautéed

2 Tbsp. green pepper, chopped and sautéed

Several pinches Lawry's Seasoning Salt

Oil for frying

2 eggs, optional

SERVES **1**

SERVING SUGGESTION:
Somers Bay Café serves a special blend of coffee from Montana Coffee Traders called Somers Bay Special Brew. Enjoy your own cup of coffee with your skillet!

Heat oil in large frying pan. Add potatoes to oil, tossing gently then add seasoning salt. Cook until brown and crispy, approximately 10 minutes, stirring occasionally.

Add the rest of the ingredients to the potatoes except eggs. Cover pan with lid to melt the cheese. Serve the skillet alone or with toast and eggs cooked to liking.

THE WORT HOTEL'S FAMOUS MEATLOAF

THE WORT HOTEL • JACKSON, WYOMING

*Andrew Smith, a food historian, mentioned that "the first recorded recipe for the modern American meatloaf is from the late 1870s." **Bon Appetit** captures, in an article entitled 'A History of Meatloaf, Long May It Reign,' the instructions for this meatloaf was to chop any cold meat on hand and add pepper, salt, onion, slices of milk-soaked bread and egg. But, the most awe-inspiring takeaway was that historically meatloaf was for breakfast rather than dinner.*

5 lbs. ground beef

6 eggs

¾ cup tomato juice

½ cup BBQ seasoning (Grill Mates recommended)

6 cups seasoned bread crumbs or croutons, crumbled

2 green bell peppers, small diced

1 white onion, small diced

SERVES 6 - 8

SERVING SUGGESTION:
Serve a couple of slices with mashed potatoes for a hearty late morning meal.

EASIEST

Place all ingredients in large bowl and mix by hand until incorporated. Mold ground beef mixture into a large log. Compact the mixture so no air pockets remain. Cook in convection oven at 325 degrees for approximately 1 hour. Confirm internal temperature of meat is 150 degrees. Let rest and slice.

RED FLANNEL HASH

THE BIG PICTURE THEATER AND CAFE • CHEF ISAAC ITEN • WAITSFIELD, VERMONT

Chef Isaac Iten of the Big Picture Theater and Cafe in the Mad River Valley loves serving this local favorite to the skiing community before hitting the slopes for the day!

4 cups corned beef, shredded

1 medium onion, diced

1 large beet, cooked and diced

2 russet potatoes, peeled, diced and cooked

3 cups kale, de-stemmed and roughly chopped

2 Tbsp. dijon mustard

1 Tbsp. Vermont maple syrup

2 eggs, prepared to liking

1 pinch black pepper

½ Tbsp. butter or oil

SERVES 2 - 3

MORE DIFFICULT

To create the Maple Mustard Glaze, mix together mustard and maple syrup.

In a large skillet, heat butter or oil and add onions. Cook until translucent then add corned beef and potatoes. Once corned beef is starting to crisp, add beets and kale. Stir and sauté until all ingredients are warm. Portion hash on a plate, drizzle Maple Mustard Glaze over hash, top with two eggs (sunny side up is a local favorite) and black pepper.

SERVING SUGGESTION:
Enjoy while noticing the beautiful blend of colors and flavors that come together for an exciting and delicious variant on traditional corned beef hash.

PACIFIC BENNY

RED'S IN RAMSAY • CALGARY, ALBERTA, CANADA

Guests feel right at home with Ramsay's urban vibe, fresh markets, creative professionals, and heritage character. Red's in Ramsay serves all-day breakfast and 'Build Your Own Burger' bar.

2 eggs, poached

English muffin, sliced and toasted

Smoked salmon, sliced

⅛ red onion, sliced

1 tsp. capers

Hollandaise sauce, store bought or home-make a favorite recipe

Splash vinegar

SERVES 1

SERVING SUGGESTION:
This Pacific Benny is served with hash browns at Red's in Ramsay.

EASIEST

In a large shallow skillet, simmer 2 - 3" water and a splash of vinegar. Slide room temperature eggs into the simmering water. Spoon some hot water over each to set the top. Poach for 4 minutes then remove with a slotted spoon and place on a paper towel.

Place sliced salmon and poached eggs atop toasted English muffins. Garnish with red onions, capers and hollandaise sauce.

SWEET REGIS SCRAMBLE

CAFÉ REGIS • CHEF LOIDA HARDIN • RED LODGE, MONTANA

A breakfast and brunch restaurant in Red Lodge, Café Regis is a relaxed locale for hearty American plates with a patio and an organic garden. The coffee is Fair Trade, the eggs are from cage-free chickens, and Café Regis uses organic and locally sourced food, including from their own gardens.

4 links of maple sausages, cooked

1 Tbsp. red peppers, chopped

1 Tbsp. yellow peppers, chopped

1 Tbsp. orange peppers, chopped

1 Tbsp. onion, chopped

4 eggs

1 Tbsp. canola oil

SERVES 2

EASIEST Chop all peppers and onion and slice sausages. To a sauté pan, add oil and cook peppers, onions and sausage until tender, about three minutes. Whisk eggs in a bowl and add to pan. Scramble until just done.

HOMEMADE HASH BROWNS

1 large russet potato

1 – 2 Tbsp. olive oil

Salt and pepper to taste

One day before enjoying, boil one large potato, until halfway done. Refrigerate overnight. Shred the potato and cook in olive oil until crispy. Add salt and pepper to taste.

SERVING SUGGESTION:
Serve scramble with Homemade Hash Browns.

LEONORA SHORT RIB HASH

LEONORA AT THE SEBASTIAN • CHEF TYSON PETERSON • VAIL, COLORADO

Set in the heart of Vail Village, just off the pedestrian corridor, Leonora offers an inviting dining experience inspired by the French Alps, Spanish Pyrenees and the Colorado Rockies. Leonora uses only the finest fresh, local and organic ingredients to create breakfast that leaves the guest fueled.

1 lb. short rib or pot roast, shredded

BBQ sauce, store bought or home-make a favorite recipe, optional

2 potatoes, baked

1 handful spinach

1 onion, chopped

3 Tbsp. butter

1 cup sauce, from cooking short rib or pot roast

8 large eggs

2 red Fresno chilies, thinly sliced

Salt and pepper to taste

Herbs of your choice, for garnish

SERVES 4

Follow a favorite pot roast recipe, or add meat with 1 bottle BBQ sauce and 1 cup water to a slow cooker. Cook for 4 - 6 hours until fork tender. Reserve sauce. Leftovers from the night before may be used.

Bake potatoes in foil at 400 degrees until tender, about 1 ¼ hour. Remove potatoes from oven and chill in refrigerator until cooled. Dice into cubes the size of large grapes. Chop onion and set aside. Heat largest sauté pan over medium-high heat then add butter and cook until foamy and melted. Add potato cubes to hot butter and crisp. Add onions and cook until soft, add sliced chilies, precooked pot roast and 1 cup leftover sauce. Cook until warm. Add spinach on top and wilt. If pan has a lid, steam on low-medium heat. Once spinach has wilted, add salt and pepper to taste.

To finish the dish, cook eggs to liking. Sunny-side up is recommended, but scrambled is delicious too. In a bowl or on a plate, serve ample hash and top with eggs.

SERVING SUGGESTION:
Garnish with sliced red Fresno chilies and soft herbs.

NORWEGIAN POTATO & BACON PANCAKE
with Poached Eggs, Jarlsberg Cheese Sauce, & Cranberry Relish

STEIN ERIKSEN LODGE • CHEF ZANE HOLMQUIST • PARK CITY, UTAH

This is one of the first dishes that Chef Holmquist created at Stein Eriksen Lodge in 2000. Chef Zane had used a similar potato cake recipe for special events but never on a menu, with the idea originating from a dish of his Swedish grandmother made on Sundays. A few weeks after it was placed on the Stein Eriksen menu, Mr. Eriksen exclaimed love for the dish and that it was one of the best breakfasts he had experienced at the hotel. It's remained on the menu for breakfast ever since. The tart cranberry relish lightens the intense flavor of the Jarlsberg cheese – both highlight the star of the dish, the potato cake.

2 Idaho potatoes, par-boiled, peeled and grated

½ small yellow onion, diced small

4 bacon strips, cooked and diced

1 egg white

1 tsp. all purpose flour

1 tsp. fresh chives, chopped

1 tsp. fresh Italian parsley, chopped

1 tsp. kosher salt

½ tsp. ground fresh black pepper

6 – 8 eggs, for assembly

½ tsp. green onions, chopped, for garnish

Jarlsberg Cheese Sauce, see recipe

Cranberry Relish, see recipe

SERVES 6 – 8

SERVING SUGGESTION:
Top the entire dish with chopped green onions.

 MORE DIFFICULT

Boil potatoes in salted water for 12 minutes; cool to room temperature, peel and grate. Peel and small-dice onion. Cook bacon and dice to similar size as onions. Reserve some bacon fat. Combine potatoes, onion and bacon. Half whip egg white; fold into potato mixture.

Mix until just combined flour, chives, parsley, salt and pepper into potato combination. Potatoes should keep grated texture. Heat reserved bacon fat in large sauté pan or on pancake griddle. Using a ¼ cup scoop, drop the potato mixture onto the heated pan or griddle. Cook until lightly browned on both sides, approximately 3 - 4 minutes per side.

Poach one egg per person, until desired doneness. Place poached egg on potato pancake. Add 4 Tbsp. Jarlsberg Cheese Sauce over egg. Garnish plate with 1 Tbsp. Cranberry Relish.

JARLSBERG CHEESE SAUCE

1 cup heavy cream

¼ cup whole milk

2 tsp. corn starch

4 tsp. cold water

2 cups Jarlsberg cheese, grated

¼ tsp. kosher salt

¼ tsp. white pepper

1 bunch fresh thyme

1 pinch nutmeg, grated

Simmer cream and milk with fresh thyme bundle.

Mix corn starch and water together. Add corn starch slurry to simmering liquid, making sure it boils. Slowly add grated Jarlsberg cheese and continually whip until smooth sauce-like consistency. Add salt, white pepper and nutmeg. Remove thyme bundle. Keep sauce warm until ready to serve.

CRANBERRY RELISH

1 ½ cups whole fresh cranberries

1 cup granulated sugar

½ orange, zested and juiced

1 pinch kosher salt

2 Tbsp. Aquavit

Mix cranberries, sugar, orange zest and juice, and salt together in a bowl. Place in a thick-bottomed saucepan; bring to a low simmer. Add Aquavit and stir occasionally for 12 minutes, or until mixture is a jam-like consistency.

THE QUINTESSENTIAL CALIFORNIA OMELETTE

SQUEEZE IN • TRUCKEE, CALIFORNIA

The Squeeze In tagline is "the best omelettes on the planet." And, with over 10 successful locations ranging from ski towns to downtowns, their word should be completely trusted as they have been praised in numerous press outlets for their omelettes.

4 whole fresh eggs, beaten (if using whites, use 6 whites instead of 4 whole eggs – saving 20 grams of fat)

6 oz. white wine sauce (white wine with a dash of soybean oil)

1 cup mushrooms, freshly sliced

½ avocado, spoon slice 8 large pieces

3 strips bacon, cooked crisp and chopped

2 oz. Monterey jack cheese, shredded

S ERVES 1 - 2

Sauté mushrooms and avocado in white wine mixture, bring to a quick simmer for 3 - 4 minutes. Cover and let sit. Heat a lightly coated 8" omelette pan with nonstick cooking spray (using cooking spray instead of butter produces a much fluffier and healthier final product). Add beaten eggs or egg whites and roll around the pan edges. When nearly no liquid remains, flip omelette over in the pan. (A toss and catch method assures there is no liquid or runny eggs inside the omelette). Turn off the flame, sprinkle cheese on one side of the omelette (all ingredients will be added to the one side, because the omelette will be folded). Use sauté pan lid to drain remaining sauce from mushroom and avocado pan. Lay mushrooms and avocados over cheese then add bacon. Fold omelette onto a plate.

SERVING SUGGESTION:
Enjoy this omelette, as it's the most popular one from the Squeeze In menu. Also known as the Racy Tracy.

TARA'S BENEDICT SALAD

SILVER FORK LODGE AND RESTAURANT • BRIGHTON, UTAH

"Comfort food at its finest," writes City Weekly.

12 whole eggs, poached

10 - 12 oz. ham, sliced into 12 small triangular pieces

12 oz. arugula

32 oz. hash browns

Pinch cayenne

Pinch salt

Pinch sugar

1 Tbsp. oil

Hollandaise Sauce, see recipe

SERVES 6

MORE DIFFICULT

In a skillet over medium heat, cook ham slices until warm. Turn a griddle to medium-high heat and coat griddle with oil. Spread hash browns around griddle, about 1" thick. Fry hash browns until golden brown and crispy. While hash browns are cooking, poach 12 eggs by simmering a large sauce pan of water. Carefully crack eggs into water and cook 3-5 minutes. Remove eggs with a slotted spoon and drain on paper towels.

On 6 plates, divide hash browns equally. Layer arugula on top of hash browns, 2 slices ham each, 2 poached eggs each and top with a dollop of Hollandaise Sauce.

SERVING SUGGESTION:
Enjoy this 'salad version' of an
Eggs Benedict.

HOLLANDAISE SAUCE

6 egg yolks

1 lemon, juiced

1 lb. butter

Pinch cayenne

Pinch salt

Pinch sugar

Heat butter in microwave until boiling, about 4 minutes. Let butter settle so milk solids fall to the bottom and separate from clarified butter on top. Add all ingredients except butter into a mixing bowl and whisk over a simmering pot of water on low heat until the sauce begins to thicken. Remove from heat before eggs scramble. When butter has separated, slowly pour clarified butter into egg mixture, whisking the entire time, until a thick sauce forms.

PANZANELLA SALAD

FEED CAFÉ • BOZEMAN, MONTANA

The Panzanella Salad is a popular item at Feed Café for both breakfast and lunch. It's a healthy yet indulgent combination of interesting textures and flavors with the spicy arugula, crunchy sourdough, rich bacon and salty feta brought together by the tangy Sun-dried Tomato Vinaigrette; it is made only better by topping with a perfectly cooked sunny side up egg.

4 cups arugula, washed and dried

4 slices good sourdough bread

4 slices bacon

½ cup feta cheese, crumbled and divided in half

4 eggs, cooked sunny side up

2 Tbsp. olive oil

Sun-dried Tomato Vinaigrette, see recipe

SERVES 4

 MORE DIFFICULT

Preheat oven to 350 degrees. Dice sourdough slices and scatter on a sheet pan. Toast until crisp, golden and browning on edges. Remove from the oven and let cool. Increase oven to 400 degrees.

Line a sheet pan with parchment paper and cook bacon until browned and crispy, approximately 15 - 20 minutes. Remove from oven, cool and crumble into bite-sized pieces.

Just before serving, combine arugula, bread, bacon and ½ feta in a large mixing bowl. Add ¼ cup Sun-dried Tomato Vinaigrette and toss gently. Add more dressing to taste. Warm a large non-stick skillet over medium heat, add olive oil and fry eggs to liking, sunny side up is preferred. Assemble salads in bowls and top each with a fried egg and 1 Tbsp. feta cheese.

SERVING SUGGESTION:
Enjoy this salad for breakfast, brunch or lunch.

SUN-DRIED TOMATO VINAIGRETTE

¼ cup sun-dried tomatoes

1 Tbsp. shallots, minced

1 Tbsp. garlic, minced

¼ cup basil, chopped

¼ cup red wine vinegar

1 tsp. honey

¼ cup olive oil

¼ cup canola oil

Salt and pepper to taste

Pour boiling water over sun-dried tomatoes in a heatproof bowl, enough to cover them completely. Soak for 20 minutes then drain. Add all ingredients except oils to blender and blend until smooth. Slowly add oils to tomato mixture to emulsify.

Taste and adjust seasoning as needed.

SUMMER POACHED EGGS
with Arugula, Mascarpone and Lemon Butter Sauce

TUCKER HILL INN • WAITSFIELD, VERMONT

Breakfast defines the Tucker Hill Inn. Guests enjoy the "slippers on a Sunday morning" feeling, the smell of freshly perked coffee filling the air and the anticipation of an artisan-crafted main breakfast entree.

2 slices Tuscan bread, grilled

¼ cup mascarpone cheese

½ cup arugula

2 slices country ham

2 eggs, poached

Lemon Butter Sauce, see recipe

SERVES 1 – 2

 EASIEST

Spread mascarpone cheese on top of grilled bread slices. Grill ham slices to warm. Place ham on top of cheese and add arugula. Top each slice with a poached egg. Ladle Lemon Butter Sauce on top of eggs.

LEMON BUTTER SAUCE

½ cup butter, melted

1 lemon, juiced

Splash white wine

Pinch salt

¼ cup heavy cream

Whip ingredients together. Reserve.

SERVING SUGGESTION:
Relish this breakfast dish knowing it is the favorite of Tucker Hill Inn's summer guests.

LOBSTER BENEDICT

THE 'DACK SHACK • LAKE PLACID, NEW YORK

This "high-end roadside diner," as co-owner Holly Healy fondly refers to The 'Dack Shack, is noted by SpoonUniversity.com as one of the "10 Places to Eat in Lake Placid Before You Die".

1 lb. lobster meat, claws and knuckles

1 small shallot, minced

1 stalk celery, finely diced

2 tsp. tarragon, finely chopped

½ cup Hellman's mayo

Salt and pepper to taste

4 egg yolks

6 Tbsp. lemon juice, freshly squeezed

1 ½ lemons, zested

Pinch white pepper

Pinch salt

½ cup + 5 Tbsp. unsalted butter, melted

8 eggs

4 English muffins, toasted and buttered

SERVES 4

SERVING SUGGESTION:
Sprinkle with a dash of cayenne pepper and sliced green onions.

 MORE DIFFICULT Make lobster salad by combining lobster meat, shallot, celery, zest from ½ lemon, 3 Tbsp. lemon juice, tarragon, mayo and salt and pepper to taste. Set aside.

In a clean glass or metal bowl, whisk egg yolks and 1 Tbsp. lemon juice vigorously until blended, add zest from 1 lemon, pepper and salt. Place bowl over pot of simmering water. Be careful not to let bowl touch water. Whisk constantly until eggs start to thicken. Don't scramble. Slowly drizzle in ½ cup melted butter whisking until thick. Taste and adjust for seasoning. Keep sauce warm.

Poach 8 eggs in shallow pan of simmering water, seasoned with 2 Tbsp. lemon juice. Toast and butter 4 English muffins. Keep warm.

Place lobster salad in sauté pan with 3 Tbsp. melted butter and toss just to warm. Place 2 oz. lobster salad on each English muffin half, top with poached egg and sauce.

BREAKFAST QUICHE AT BRASS LANTERN INN

BRASS LANTERN INN • STOWE, VERMONT

This quiche is the most requested at Brass Lantern Inn; repeat customers request the dish upon reserving online or over the phone.

9" pastry shell, unbaked, store bought or home-make a favorite recipe

8 slices applewood smoked bacon, cooked, drained and crumbled

1 cup spinach, chopped

2 scallions, chopped

2 cups quality Swiss cheese, shredded

¼ cup Gruyere cheese, shredded

4 large eggs, lightly beaten

1 cup whole milk

¾ cup light cream

1 Tbsp. all purpose flour

⅛ tsp. baking powder

½ tsp. salt

⅛ tsp. nutmeg, freshly ground

Herb Roasted Red Skin Potatoes, see recipe

SERVES 6

MORE DIFFICULT

Preheat oven to 450 degrees. Bake perforated pastry shell for 7 minutes or until lightly brown. Remove baked pastry shell from oven and immediately spread ¼ cup Swiss cheese on pastry shell. Reduce oven temperature to 325 degrees. In alternating layers add bacon (reserve 2 Tbsp. for top), all cheeses, all scallions and all spinach. In a medium bowl, combine lightly beaten eggs, milk, light cream, flour, baking powder, salt and nutmeg. Pour egg mixture into pastry shell and sprinkle with reserved bacon.

Bake at 325 degrees for 40 - 50 minutes. Do not over cook; quiche will continue to cook after removing from oven. Remove and let stand for 10 minutes, lightly cover with foil and let quiche rest for another 15 minutes before serving.

HERB ROASTED RED SKIN POTATOES

12 – 15 red potatoes, quartered

⅛ cup olive oil

Garlic salt to taste

Pepper, freshly ground to taste

⅛ cup fresh rosemary, cut sprigs

⅛ cup fresh sage, chopped

Wash and dry potatoes, coat potatoes lightly and evenly with olive oil, arrange in a baking dish, and sprinkle with garlic salt, freshly ground pepper, rosemary and sage. Cover with foil tightly and bake at 325 degrees for 2 hours.

SERVING SUGGESTION:
Serve a generous slice with Herb Roasted Red Skin Potatoes.

GREEN MOUNTAIN INN'S AVOCADO TOAST

GREEN MOUNTAIN INN • STOWE, VERMONT

For more than 180 years, the Green Mountain Inn has captivated travelers from around the world. Located on Main Street in the heart of historic Stowe, the rich history and overwhelming beauty entices visitors to return.

1 avocado, pitted and mashed

1 Tbsp. lime juice

1 slice honey oat bread, toasted

2 eggs, cooked any style

2 slices bacon, applewood smoked and cooked

¼ cup heirloom tomatoes, diced

1 clove fresh garlic, chopped

1 Tbsp. cilantro, chopped

Salt and pepper to taste

¼ cup Vermont cheddar, crumbled

Sour cream

SERVES 1- 2

SERVING SUGGESTION:
Enjoy the avocado toast as a perfect start to the day.

EASIEST

Assemble heirloom tomato salad by combining tomatoes, garlic, cilantro and salt and pepper to taste. For avocado spread, mash and season with lime juice, salt and pepper. Spread avocados on toasted honey oat bread. Top with eggs cooked any style, bacon, tomato salad, cheddar and a drizzle of sour cream.

ELEMENTS HAM & BRIE STUFFED FRENCH TOAST

ELEMENTS URBAN TAPAS PARLOUR • WHISTLER, BRITISH COLUMBIA, CANADA

Elements Urban Tapas Parlour has been voted the best tapas in the annual Whistler Pique News magazine since opening in 2005. The restaurant is also a close second behind Wild Wood Pacific Bistro for Best Breakfast, but being similarly owned, and both included in Ski Town Brunch, it's a win-win!

1 loaf French bread, uncut

6 slices ham

1 large wheel brie cheese, cut into 6 slices

4 eggs

2 Tbsp. milk

4 Tbsp. butter

Canadian maple syrup

Powdered sugar

SERVES 3

Preheat oven to 400 degrees. Cut a 6-inch piece out of the loaf at the bottom and pull inside bread out, but save 6-inch outside crust. Roll brie inside of ham slices and place rolls inside hollowed bread. Then, plug the loaf with reserved crust.

Cut 6 diagonal slices. Prepare egg wash by beating eggs with milk then dip slices in egg wash, coating all sides. Melt butter in oven-safe skillet, brown slices, and cook at 400 degrees for 15 minutes. Serve 2 slices per plate and dust with powdered sugar.

SERVING SUGGESTION:
Serve with real Canadian maple syrup.

HUEVOS RANCHEROS
with Cumin Lime Cream and Salsa

HUCKLEBERRY HILL BED AND BREAKFAST • SANDPOINT, IDAHO

Huckleberry Hill's flavorful and creative cuisine is showcased in this favorite breakfast dish - Huevos Rancheros with Cumin Lime Cream and Salsa. To accommodate dietary restrictions, use all corn, gluten-free tortillas. This dish can also be made dairy-free by substituting avocado for sour cream in the Cumin Lime Cream and eliminating cheese.

12 farm fresh large eggs

1 ½ cups refried beans

1 ½ cups Cotija cheese, crumbled

12 6 – 8" corn and flour blend tortillas

Cumin Lime Cream, see recipe

Salsa, see recipe

SERVES 6

MORE DIFFICULT

Spread ¼ cup refried beans on 6 tortillas and sprinkle ¼ cup cheese on top. Place plain tortillas atop covered ones – making a sandwich. Cook in heated skillet or griddle, flipping to toast each side. Place toasted tortillas on cutting board and cook eggs (sunny side up is traditional, but cook to liking).

While eggs cook, cut each "quesadilla" into 5 pieces. Make a swoosh of Cumin Lime Cream on the plate and arrange tortillas. Top with eggs, then Salsa.

SERVING SUGGESTION:
Serve with Cumin Lime Cream, Salsa, and a hot sauce. Chorizo sausage, avocado, and garden fresh tomatoes also pair well with this dish.

CUMIN LIME CREAM

1 cup sour cream

¼ cup lime juice, freshly squeezed

1 – 2 limes, zested

1 tsp. cumin powder

½ tsp. paprika

Salt and pepper to taste

Whisk all ingredients together. Reserve.

SALSA

2 large fresh tomatoes, diced

½ small onion, small diced

1 clove garlic, minced

½ - 1 fresh jalapeño, minced

1 tsp. chili powder

Salt and pepper to taste

For a milder salsa, remove seeds of jalapeño. If spicier is preferred, add seeds. Incorporate all ingredients.

BLACKENED SALMON

THE INN • CHEF JASON CHARTRAND • MONTGOMERY CENTER, VERMONT

Discerning guests will enjoy the equal parts ski chalet, gentlemen's club and hunting lodge that The Inn offers. The restaurant serves new American cuisine by Chef Jason Chartrand who focuses on hyper-seasonal ingredients. Blackened Salmon is his signature dish.

1 lb. wild caught Alaskan salmon, skinned and pin bones removed by butcher

1 spaghetti squash

4 Tbsp. pesto, store bought or home-make a favorite recipe

½ cup heavy cream

2 Tbsp. Cajun seasoning

2 Tbsp. blackening seasoning

1 carrot

2 Tbsp. vegetable or avocado oil

SERVES 2

MORE DIFFICULT

Divide salmon into two portions. Remove outside skin of carrot. Peel carrot, reserving the long peels. Place carrot ribbons in a bowl of ice cold water. Cut in half and remove center seeds of spaghetti squash, place on plate and cover with plastic wrap; microwave on high for 8-9 minutes. Let squash cool then shred with a fork. Heat 1 cup squash in a small saute pan with pesto and a little water until water has evaporated.

Meanwhile, in a small saucepan heat heavy cream and Cajun seasoning and simmer until slightly thickened. Coat salmon filets with blackening seasoning, heat oil in nonstick 10" pan until smoking and carefully place salmon in pan. Cook 1 minute, then carefully turn using a fish spatula and cook for 2 minutes for medium rare.

In two large pasta bowls, ladle Cajun cream sauce to cover bottoms. Place equal amounts of spaghetti squash in the center, then salmon on top of squash. Make 2 balls with carrot ribbons and set atop salmon filets.

SERVING SUGGESTION:
Enjoy this visual masterpiece with a companion.

WILD SALMON WRAP

CAFÉ REGIS • CHEF LOIDA HARDIN • RED LODGE, MONTANA

Jodie and Judy Christensen purchased Café Regis in 2017. Having owned and sold another restaurant in Red Lodge for 24 years, they wanted to try their hands at a breakfast and lunch place. They lovingly refer to it as their "retirement restaurant".

8 oz. salmon filet

1 cup fresh baby spinach, chopped

¼ cup Swiss cheese

¼ cup cucumber, chopped

2 large flour tortillas

¼ cup mayonnaise

1 Tbsp. sweet pickle relish

SERVES **2**

SERVING SUGGESTION:
Serve with fruit salad.

EASIEST

Saute, grill or bake salmon until done. Warm tortillas and spread mixture of mayonnaise and pickle relish on tortillas. Fill tortillas with spinach, cheese, salmon and cucumber. Fold as wraps and cut in half.

CHICKEN FRIED STEAK EGGS BENEDICT

TOOLOULOU'S • CHEF STEVE SMYTHE • BANFF, ALBERTA, CANADA

Tooloulou's introduced itself to the downtown Banff dining scene in October 2012. A casual and intimate fifty seat restaurant, Tooloulou's offers a Cajun Creole inspired flair alongside a touch of Canadian Rocky Mountain infusion. Chef Steve Smythe embraces the opportunity to merge his love of hearty home-style cooking that combines southern and Louisiana flavors with true Canadian character.

2 lbs. beef cube steak or bottom round steak

2 cups all purpose flour

2 tsp. baking powder

1 tsp. baking soda

1 tsp. black pepper

¾ tsp. salt

1 egg

1 Tbsp. hot sauce

2 cloves garlic, minced

3 cups vegetable shortening for frying

1 ½ cups buttermilk

Quick Sweet Cornbread, see recipe

Cajun Blender Hollandaise Sauce, see recipe

4 eggs, poached

BBQ sauce, store bought or home-make a favorite recipe

Green onions, for garnish

SERVES 4

 MOST DIFFICULT

Cut steak into ½ lb. portions and pound steaks to ¼" thickness. Place flour in a shallow bowl. In a separate bowl, mix baking powder, baking soda, pepper and salt then add buttermilk, egg, hot sauce and garlic. Dredge each steak in flour, then in batter and again in flour. Melt shortening in a deep cast iron pan to hot (325 degrees). Fry steaks until golden brown (3-5 minutes per side). Drain on paper towels. Poach eggs.

Toast or grill 4 slices Quick Sweet Cornbread. Place one chicken fried steak on top of a cornbread slice. Add a poached egg on top of chicken fried steak. Top everything with Cajun Blender Hollandaise Sauce and drizzle with BBQ sauce.

QUICK SWEET CORNBREAD

1 ½ cups cornmeal

2 ½ cups milk

2 cups all purpose flour

1 Tbsp. baking powder

1 tsp. salt

⅔ cup white sugar

2 eggs

½ cup vegetable oil

Preheat oven to 400 degrees. Combine cornmeal and milk, let stand for 5 minutes. Grease a 9 x 13" baking pan. Whisk together flour, baking powder, salt and sugar. Mix in cornmeal mixture, eggs and oil until smooth. Pour batter into greased pan and bake for 30-35 minutes.

SERVING SUGGESTION:
Sprinkle with chopped green onions.

CAJUN BLENDER HOLLANDAISE SAUCE

3 egg yolks

1 Tbsp. fresh lemon juice

½ tsp. salt

⅛ tsp. cayenne

10 Tbsp. unsalted butter

Melt butter slowly. In a blender at medium, blend egg yolks, lemon juice, salt and cayenne until light in color, about 30 seconds. Lower blender speed and drizzle in butter. Adjust salt and lemon juice to taste. If hollandaise is too thick, add a little warm water.

CHILE RELLENO CASSEROLE

A'TAVOLA GOURMET MARKETPLACE • CHEF LISA PETERSON • BOISE, IDAHO

Lisa Peterson's a'Tavola Gourmet Marketplace is a culmination of a lifetime spent pursuing a passion for fine foods, mentoring a gifted and spirited team of like-minded people, and enjoying the relationships cultivated with her family and friends sharing these passions. Along with Lisa, the Peterson family is now able to welcome friends and guests to their table to celebrate food with them in all its forms by feasting together.

4 - 7 oz. cans whole green chiles, drained, rinsed and patted dry*

1 ½ cups cheddar cheese, shredded

1 ½ cups monterey jack cheese, shredded

5 large eggs

1 ½ cups heavy cream

¼ cup flour

1 ½ tsp. dry mustard

1 ½ tsp. chili powder

1 ½ tsp. baking powder

¼ tsp. salt

¼ tsp. pepper

½ cup cilantro, chopped

½ cup black olives, sliced

½ bunch green onions, chopped

1 tomato, seeded and chopped

* a'Tavola uses fresh roasted pasilla chiles

SERVES 8

EASIEST

Preheat oven to 350 degrees. Spray a 9 x 13 baking dish with nonstick cooking spray. Remove chiles from can, split in half lengthwise, and rinse. Pat dry. Add eggs, heavy cream, flour, dry mustard, chili powder, baking powder, salt, and pepper to a medium bowl and beat until smooth. Arrange a single layer of chiles in prepared baking dish and cover the bottom completely. Sprinkle 1/3 of cheese evenly over peppers. Repeat layering 2 more times. Pour egg mixture over chiles and rest for 10 minutes for even distribution. Sprinkle cilantro, olives, green onions, and tomatoes (and more cheese, if desired) on top and bake uncovered for 30 - 40 minutes, or until center is set. Let stand 10 minutes before cutting.

SERVING SUGGESTION:
Enjoy a portion of this casserole with a refreshing fruit salad.

FALL HASH

SWIFT CREEK CAFÉ • CHEF CHRISTIAN MORENO • WHITEFISH, MONTANA

Swift Creek Café is a place of character, art, family and community, just as much as it's about food. The Moreno Halphen family draws on their extensive 80 years of experience of being in the food and coffee industry. The family tradition is carried forward by award-winning Executive Chef, Christian Moreno. He earned a degree from the top French pastry program, "Ecole Nationale Supérieure de Pâtisserie" in Yssingeaux, France.

12 oz. butternut squash, peeled, diced large, and roasted

1 bunch Lacinato kale, stemmed and cut in chiffonade

3 russet potatoes, quartered and sliced ¼" thick

4 oz. chicken thighs, braised in butter and pulled

3 oz. chanterelle mushrooms, cleaned and roasted

1 Sweet Tango apple, julienned

2 shallots, sliced paper thin

2 Tbsp. bacon raisin jam or another jam of choice

1 egg, fried sunny side up

1 lb. + 6 Tbsp. butter

2 sprigs thyme

Salt and pepper to taste

Micro greens, for garnish

¼ cup flour, seasoned with salt and pepper

SERVES 1 – 2

Roast butternut squash at 375 degrees with 2 Tbsp. butter and 1 sprig thyme until cooked through. Cool, toss with kale and set aside. Slice potatoes and simmer in water until cooked; set aside. Season chicken with salt and pepper, add 1 lb. chopped butter, cover with foil and cook at 225 degrees until fork tender. Pull chicken and chill. Clean and roast mushrooms in 2 Tbsp. butter, 1 sprig thyme, salt, and pepper. Set aside. Dredge paper-thin shallots in flour seasoned with salt and pepper and fry at 350 until crisp but not burnt. Brown 2 Tbsp. butter in a pan on the stovetop then brown potatoes and squash and toss with roasted ingredients. Fry egg in a pan. Warm jam and spread on a plate; top the jam with hash and place the fried egg on top with shallots and julienned apples.

SERVING SUGGESTION:
Top finished creation with micro greens.

THE CABIN GRILL'S ADIRONDACK SKILLET

THE CABIN GRILL AT HOTEL NORTH WOODS • LAKE PLACID, NEW YORK

Hotel North Woods, downtown Lake Placid's premier historic hotel provides quintessential access to the heart of Lake Placid, the 'Crown Jewel of the Adirondacks High Peaks Region'.

2 Tbsp. canola oil

½ cup red potato home fries, cooked and chopped

⅛ cup onions, chopped

⅛ cup green peppers, chopped

⅓ cup chorizo sausage, ground

¼ cup black beans

3 farm fresh eggs, beaten

½ cup cheddar jack cheese, shredded

½ cup fresh pico de gallo

⅛ cup sour cream

¼ avocado, peeled and sliced

SERVES 1

Preheat oven to 350 degrees. Heat oil in an oven-safe skillet on medium-high and cook home fries, onions and peppers until golden brown and crispy on edges. Add chorizo sausage and sauté until brown. Add black beans, mix and reduce heat to medium. Add beaten eggs and stir to combine. Top with cheese and bake at 350 degrees until cheese melts. Remove from oven.

SERVING SUGGESTION:
Garnish with pico de gallo, sour cream and avocado.

CHORIZO BREAKFAST TACOS
with Ranchero Beans

COAL CREEK GRILL AND FOREST QUEEN HOTEL • CHEF DOUGLAS DODD •
CRESTED BUTTE, COLORADO

Coal Creek Grill is a favorite brunch spot for both locals and visitors of Crested Butte. Whether starting out with a warm sunny day on the creekside patio or getting ready to ski on a snowy morning, Chorizo Breakfast Tacos are a great way to start the day. Located in Southwestern Colorado, Coal Creek Grill's Colorado cuisine is influenced by the local mountains with a hint of the Southwest.

1 Tbsp. butter

3 large eggs

3 4 ½" flour tortillas

1 oz. pepper jack cheese, shredded

2 oz. chorizo sausage, cooked and crumbled

3 Tbsp. salsa

3 Tbsp. sour cream

¼ avocado, sliced

1 cup Ranchero Beans, see recipe

SERVES 1 - 2

Melt butter in nonstick sauté pan over medium heat. Cook chorizo until hot. Beat eggs in a bowl and add to sauté pan with chorizo. Scramble. Warm flour tortillas on griddle over medium heat. Divide cheese and add to center of warm tortillas then spoon on scrambled eggs. Top tacos with salsa and sour cream. Garnish each taco with the avocado slices.

SERVING SUGGESTION:
Serve with Ranchero Beans on the side.

RANCHERO BEANS

1 15 oz. can white or great northern beans, drained

4 Tbsp. carrot, diced

4 Tbsp. celery, diced

4 Tbsp. onion, diced

1 tsp. garlic, minced

3 oz. chorizo sausage, cooked and crumbled

½ oz. cider vinegar

2 oz. BBQ Sauce, store bought or home-make a favorite recipe

4 oz. water

2 Tbsp. cilantro, chopped

½ Tbsp. chili powder

1 tsp. ground cumin

1 tsp. ground coriander

In a medium pot, sauté chorizo sausage, carrots, celery, onions and garlic until vegetables are tender. Add remaining ingredients. Cook at low simmer for 10 minutes until sauce has reached desired consistency.

THE BREAKFAST POUTINE

STONESEDGE KITCHEN • CHEF BOBBY AND CHEF TAIT • WHISTLER, BRITISH COLUMBIA, CANADA

Chef Bobby is as Canadian as they come, he always wears plaid, he believes everything is better with bacon and has eaten so much maple syrup he's sure it's running through his veins. Chef Tait is originally Australian but a new Canadian citizen. To showcase this Canadian beauty, the chefs tried many versions and finally the breakfast poutine was born! Stonesedge has an amazing view of the surrounding mountains and has an awesome brunch vibe. Stonesedge Kitchen believes that a night out deserves a fantastic brunch to get you back up and going!

1 cup potatoes, a medley of favorites

¼ cup cheese curds

2 Tbsp. Red Pepper and Onion Relish, see recipe

Handful fresh spinach

2 eggs

2 oz. hollandaise sauce, store bought or home-make a favorite recipe

3 Tbsp. white vinegar

2 Tbsp. olive oil

4 strips bacon, cooked crispy and crumbled

Maple syrup

Montreal Steak Spice, optional

Salt and pepper to taste

SERVES 2

SERVING SUGGESTION:
Garnish with bacon!

MORE DIFFICULT

Bake bacon in a 400 degree oven until crispy. Remove from oven and brush with maple syrup. Reduce oven to 375 degrees. Cube potato medley, toss in oil, salt and pepper. Place on baking sheet, bake until golden brown and crispy. To add more spice, add Montreal Steak Spice to potatoes.

In an oven safe skillet place cooked potato medley on bottom, spread Red Pepper and Onion Relish over top. Cover with cheese curds. Bake in oven until cheese is half melted. In a pot, add 12 cups water and white vinegar and low simmer. Carefully place 2 cracked eggs into poaching water.

In a serving bowl, add spinach, cheese-covered potato mix and place poached eggs on top. Cover with hollandaise sauce to liking and top with bacon.

RED PEPPER AND ONION RELISH

2 yellow onions, thinly sliced

2 red peppers, thinly sliced

1 tsp. mustard seed

½ cup red wine vinegar

½ cup brown sugar

1 tsp. smoked paprika

Add thinly sliced onions and peppers to a hot pot with mustard seed, vinegar, brown sugar, paprika and simmer. Turn down temperature and cook for 35-40 minutes until onions are soft. Remove from heat and set aside.

DUCK AND ROOT VEGETABLE HASH
with Eggs and Sambal Aioli

BIG SLIDE BREWERY AND PUBLIC HOUSE • CHEF GREG SHERMAN • LAKE PLACID, NEW YORK

Big Slide Brewery and Public House is well-known for their brunch, so much so that it's advertised directly on the website's homepage. The Big Slide Brunch serves Chef Sherman's wonderful concoctions paired with bloody mary's, mimosas, beer and even beer cocktails.

2 7-oz. duck breasts, boneless and skin on

Salt and pepper

2 lbs. root vegetables*, small diced

1 large red pepper, small diced

1 red onion, small diced

1 tsp. Chinese 5 spice

1 tsp. cumin

1 tsp. cinnamon

4 Tbsp. butter

8 eggs, cooked to liking

Pickled Vegetables, see recipe

Aioli, see recipe

Cilantro and green onions, for garnish

SERVES 4

 MOST DIFFICULT

Score skin of duck by cutting small diamond shapes through the skin only. Pat skin dry and season with salt and pepper. Place duck breasts skin side down in a cold frying pan. On medium-high heat, cook until most of fat has melted away and skin is golden brown. Turn breasts over, cook on non-skin side until golden brown, 3-4 minutes. Turn breasts on sides and brown, 1 minute per side. Breasts should be medium. Rest off heat for 5 minutes.

In a large, heavy bottom skillet, melt butter on medium low heat. Add vegetables (*any combination of carrot, celery root, parsnip, rutabaga, potato, and/or yam) and spices, cook until vegetables soften and spices are fragrant.

Cube duck breast and mix into hash. Cook 8 eggs to liking. Divide hash among 4 plates or big bowls. Top with Pickled Vegetables, 2 eggs each and a drizzle of Aioli.

PICKLED VEGETABLES

½ cucumber, cut in half lengthwise, seeds removed, and sliced thin

½ medium carrot, peeled and cut into matchsticks

1 cup rice wine vinegar

¾ cup sugar

1 cup water

1 Tbsp. Sambal oelek chili paste

Place carrots and cucumbers in a bowl. Boil remaining ingredients then pour over vegetables. Cool in refrigerator.

SERVING SUGGESTION: Garnish with chopped cilantro and sliced green onions.

AIOLI

1 cup mayonnaise

1 Tbsp. lemon juice

1 Tbsp. Sambal oelek chili paste, plus more to taste

Mix all ingredients until smooth and creamy.

AVOCADO MOUSSE & TOMATO JAM TOAST
with Soft Poached Egg

GRAND TARGHEE RESORT • CHEF CHRISTIAN BUSTAMANTE • ALTA, WYOMING

The first ski area in Wyoming to open for the 2018 - 2019 ski season, Grand Targhee Resort celebrates its 50th anniversary in 2019.

2 slices multigrain artisan bread, toasted

4 ripe avocados

2 Tbsp. shallots, minced or micro-planed

1 lime or lemon, juiced

Salt and black pepper to taste

Tomato Jam, see recipe

2 eggs

Arugula, micro greens and/or sprouts, for garnish

SERVES 1

MORE DIFFICULT

To make the avocado mousse, cut avocados in half and remove the pit. Scoop out flesh and place in a blender along with shallots and lime or lemon juice. Blend until smooth. Remove from blender and pass through a fine-mesh strainer, adjust seasoning to taste. Place in a sealable cup and chill until ready to use.

Boil water in a medium pot then reduce heat to medium simmer. Gently place eggs in water. For soft boiled eggs, poach for 5 - 6 minutes. Once eggs have cooked, immediately place in a water bath for a minute to prevent overcooking and maintain perfect texture. Eggs should still be warm.

Place slices of toasted bread on a plate and spread liberally with avocado mousse. Top each with a copious amount of Tomato Jam and add a poached egg to the prepared slices.

SERVING SUGGESTION:
Garnish with arugula, micro greens or sprouts.

TOMATO JAM

1 ¾ lb. San Marzano tomatoes, chopped

½ onion, small diced

¼ cup sugar, light brown

¾ cup sugar, granulated

½ tsp. kosher salt

¼ tsp. coriander

3 Tbsp. champagne vinegar

½ lemon, juiced

In a medium pot, simmer all ingredients until thick, 2 - 3 hours. Remove from heat. If smoother texture is desired, puree the mixture. Portion in sealable cups and chill until ready to use.

TOMATO & KALE QUICHE DU JOUR

WOODSTOCK INN AND RESORT • WOODSTOCK, VERMONT

Presenting the Richardson's Tavern Quiche du Jour Brunch Platter, a representative of the essence of Vermont and flavor-driven plates that are showcased at Richardson's Tavern. Richardson's Tavern is located in the Woodstock Inn and Resort where thoughtful authenticity blends seamlessly with a classic resort experience for a timeless elegance.

8 oz. half and half

3 eggs

¼ cup baby kale, chopped

8 grape tomatoes, halved

Salt and pepper

SERVES 4

EASIEST

In a mixing bowl, whip eggs and half and half together until blended smooth. Add a pinch of salt and a pinch of pepper and fold. In nonstick baking cups, add equal portions of kale to each cup and 4 halves of tomato in each cup. Pour egg mixture in cups to cover kale and tomato. Bake at 325 degrees for 25 minutes until egg is setup firm to touch.

MIXED GREENS SALAD

½ cup mixed greens

¼ cucumber, sliced

4 cherry tomatoes

2 – 3 Tbsp. balsamic vinaigrette, or dressing of your choice

Mix greens with dressing and garnish with tomato and cucumber.

SERVING SUGGESTION:
Serve the quiche with Mixed Greens Salad, Meats & Cheese Arrangement and wedge of cantaloupe and mixed berries.

MEATS & CHEESE ARRANGEMENT

1 oz. prosciutto cotto, sliced

1 oz. Jasper Hill Vault #5 cheddar cheese, cubed

Recommended: use local meats and cheese for this dish. A favorite is local prosciutto cotto; a cooked prosciutto from Vermont Salumi company. For the cheese, a local cheddar cheese from Jasper Hill is a favored choice. It is a cave-aged cheddar that gives it a smooth, but robust cheddar flavor.

SWEETS:
BREADS & PASTRIES

SWEETS:
BREADS & PASTRIES
continued

LEMON SOUFFLÉ PANCAKES

ELEMENT 47 AT THE LITTLE NELL • ASPEN, COLORADO

Mornings at The Little Nell are made all the more sweet with breakfast at Element 47. Among the most notable dishes on the breakfast menu are the Lemon Soufflé Pancakes served with homemade raspberry syrup and toasted pine nuts.

DRY INGREDIENTS:

1 cup cake flour

2 Tbsp. all purpose flour

¼ cup sugar

1 tsp. baking powder

½ tsp. salt

Dash nutmeg

2 lemons, zested

WET INGREDIENTS:

1 cup ricotta cheese

½ cup buttermilk

½ cup butter, melted

1 ½ Tbsp. lemon juice

½ tsp. vanilla

2 eggs, separated

GARNISH:

Powdered sugar, for garnish

Raspberries, for garnish

Pine nuts, toasted for garnish

SERVES 2 - 4

MORE DIFFICULT

Beat egg whites until soft peaks form. Combine all dry ingredients together in one bowl and all wet ingredients in another bowl, except egg whites. Gently mix wet ingredients into dry ingredients. Do not over mix batter or pancakes will be too dense. Gently fold batter into egg whites.

Heat a large skillet or griddle to medium and grease. Spoon 2 - 3 tablespoons of batter onto the skillet and cook until bubbles have formed. Flip and cook other side until golden brown.

SERVING SUGGESTION:
Sprinkle with powdered sugar, scatter pine nuts and plate with fresh raspberries.

JULIA CHILD CREPE

THE BOOKWORM OF EDWARDS • OWNER NICOLE MAGISTRO • EDWARDS, COLORADO

The Bookworm is a community bookstore and café located in the heart of Eagle County, near Vail and Beaver Creek ski resorts. A favorite among locals and visitors, the comfortable café is best known for its literary-themed crepes, and also serves a healthy menu including salads, soups, smoothies and craft coffee.

1 cup white flour

⅙ cup sugar

Pinch salt

½ Tbsp. vegetable oil

3 eggs

2 ⅓ cups whole milk

1 jar Nutella

8 oz. fruit such as strawberries, banana or apples, thinly sliced

Powdered sugar to taste

SERVES 6 - 8

 EASIEST Add flour, sugar, salt, oil, eggs and ½ cup milk to a mixer bowl. Use paddle attachment and beat on medium high until smooth. Use a spatula to scrape the sides and bottom of the bowl. While mixer is on a low speed, slowly add another ½ cup milk and beat until incorporated. Scrape bowl thoroughly to eliminate lumps. Keeping mixer at low speed, slowly add another ⅔ cup milk, then add remaining milk and beat until incorporated. Strain batter through a fine mesh screen. Let stand for several minutes. Batter can be prepared the night before; whisk again just before use.

Heat lightly oiled griddle or nonstick pan over medium-high heat. Ladle ¼ cup batter onto griddle. Tilt pan in a circular motion so batter coats the surface evenly and starts to firm on the bottom. Cook until the bottom is light brown. Fold into half-moon shape using a thin spatula. Apply about ¼ cup Nutella to the folded crepe, spreading evenly to cover the center section. Then arrange ¼ cup thinly sliced fruit onto the spread. One at a time, fold corners toward center to create a triangular shape. Slide onto a serving plate and sprinkle with powdered sugar.

SERVING SUGGESTION:
Garnish with additional fruit, if desired. Whipped cream, Greek yogurt or chopped nuts are also pleasant additions to this dish.

RASPBERRY HUCKLEBERRY CREAM CHEESE COFFEE CAKE

STACEY CAKES • CHEF STACEY KUCY • MCCALL, IDAHO

Stacey Cakes, in downtown McCall, Idaho, has become a destination bakery for locals and tourists alike. Stacey Kucy opened her namesake bakery in 2011 after an extremely acclaimed career: degree in Baking and Pastry from the Culinary Institute of America, baking wedding cakes in Santa Fe, NM, working as assistant pastry chef at the Coyote Cafe and heading the pastry creations at Snake River Grill in Jackson, WY. The Raspberry Huckleberry Cream Cheese Coffee Cake features an abundance of raspberries from Chef Stacey's garden and huckleberries from the vast mountain region. The combination of raspberries and huckleberries lead the perfect marriage of sweet and tart in this signature cake.

7 eggs

4 cups sour cream

1 lb. butter

2 Tbsp. baking powder

1 tsp. salt

4 ⅔ cups sugar

6 cups flour

8 oz. cream cheese, room temperature

¼ cup corn starch

½ cup raspberries

½ cup huckleberries

Crumb Topping, see recipe

SERVES 12

In a small bowl, whisk 4 eggs and sour cream together. With an electric mixer fitted with paddle attachment, cream butter, baking powder and salt then mix on low for 2 - 3 minutes, until softened. Add 4 cups sugar and increase mixer up to medium for 3 - 4 minutes, until light and fluffy, scraping down the sides as needed. Turn mixer to low, add egg mixture, a few tablespoons at a time, and mix until incorporated. Add flour to butter mixture in 3 batches, mixing on low until just combined. Line cake pans with parchment paper, grease and flour. Spread batter into 2 - 8" cake pans.

Place cream cheese in mixer bowl. Using paddle attachment, mix on medium speed for 5 minutes, scraping down the sides frequently. Add 3 eggs, one at a time, fully incorporating each egg before adding another. Add ⅔ cup sugar and corn starch until ingredients are combined about 1 minute. Divide cream cheese filling between two cake pans, spreading filling over cake batter. Sprinkle raspberries and huckleberries over cream cheese filling. Divide and sprinkle Crumb Topping over berries.

Bake at 350 degrees for 45 – 60 minutes or until center of cake doesn't jiggle. Cool for 15 minutes and unmold cakes.

SERVING SUGGESTION:
Serve a generous slice of cake with fresh huckleberries and blueberries.

CRUMB TOPPING

1 ¼ cups flour

½ cup sugar

4 oz. butter, chilled

Combine flour and sugar in a bowl. Cut butter into ¼" pieces and drop into bowl of dry ingredients. Mix with fingers, working butter into flour until mixture is coarse and crumbly.

LEMON RICOTTA DUTCH BABY CAKE

DEER VALLEY GROCERY CAFÉ • PARK CITY, UTAH

A Dutch baby pancake is sometimes referred to as a German pancake, a Bismarck, or a Dutch puff. Americans may liken it to a large popover or English may compare it to a large Yorkshire pudding.

1 ½ cups all purpose flour

½ cup sugar

1 tsp. salt

2 cups milk

2 lemons, juiced and zested

⅔ cup ricotta cheese

1 tsp. vanilla

10 eggs

1 tsp. baking powder

1 cup butter

Fresh berries, your choice

MAKES 16 6-INCH DUTCH BABIES

MORE DIFFICULT

Whisk flour, baking powder, sugar and salt together. Mix together with milk, zest, juice and cheese. Add eggs one at a time, whisking after each one. Add vanilla.

Preheat oven to 425 degrees with 6-inch cast iron pan inside. For each pancake, put 1 Tbsp. of butter in hot cast iron pan and add ¾ cup of batter. Bake 8-10 minutes until golden brown.

SERVING SUGGESTION:
Top with fresh berries.

STUFFED FRENCH TOAST
with Citrus Glaze

GOLDMINER'S DAUGHTER LODGE • CHEF MARIE HEYWOOD • ALTA, UTAH

Marie Heywood is an executive chef at the Goldminer's Daughter Lodge in Alta, Utah. She has been working in the restaurant industry for more than 10 years, and even owned her own pizza parlor for a time. She enjoys the freedom and creativity that comes from cooking, and loves managing the rowdy bunch of ski bums up in Alta.

3 eggs

2 cups half and half

2 Tbsp. sugar

1 tsp. vanilla

1 tsp. cinnamon

8 - 12 slices Texas toast

Cream Cheese Filling, see recipe

Homemade Orange Syrup, see recipe

SERVES **4**

MORE DIFFICULT

Combine eggs, half and half, sugar, vanilla and cinnamon in a mixing bowl and whisk together; set aside. Dip Texas toast or thick slices of bread in batter and grill for 4 minutes per side. Remove from grill. Scoop a generous amount of the Cream Cheese Filling on one slice of French toast and spread. Place another piece of French toast on top, like a sandwich. Cut French toast in half and place on plate.

SERVING SUGGESTION:
Drizzle with delicious Homemade Orange Syrup.

CREAM CHEESE FILLING

8 oz. cream cheese, room temperature

1 tsp. lemon peel, grated

1 tsp. orange peel, grated

1 Tbsp. lemon juice

1 Tbsp. orange juice

¼ cup powdered sugar

2 Tbsp. heavy cream

In a mixing bowl with a whisk attachment, mix cream cheese for 2 - 3 minutes until smooth. Add grated peels, juices, powdered sugar, and heavy cream and whisk for 5 minutes or until fluffy.

HOMEMADE ORANGE SYRUP

1 cup sugar

¾ cup orange juice

½ cup water plus ½ cup warm water for slurry

3 Tbsp. corn starch

2 Tbsp. butter

In a pan at medium heat, whisk ½ cup water and sugar until sugar dissolves. Add orange juice and butter and whisk until incorporated. Combine ½ cup warm water and corn starch to make a slurry then add to mixture. Syrup should thicken within minutes.

TOAST OF THE MIDNIGHT SUN

JEWEL LAKE BED AND BREAKFAST • ANCHORAGE, ALASKA

With a love for Alaska and all things breakfast, running a B & B in Anchorage is the perfect fit for Jess and Rob Muller - together they run Jewel Lake Bed and Breakfast. The Muller's work Alaskan cuisine into their menu by serving locally made reindeer sausage, sourdough bread and fresh blueberries alongside their house made jams and butters. The Toast of the Midnight Sun is a favorite twist on classic French toast casserole. It is conveniently prepped the day before and is easily modified to accommodate dietary restrictions or highlight local and seasonal fruit. Recipe pictured was made with cream cheese, brown sugar, frozen blueberries (rinsed to avoid purple tint to final dish), almond milk and caramel baking chips.

1 16-oz. loaf of sourdough or French bread (day old bread works well), cut into 1-inch cubes

8 oz. cream cheese (optional)

⅔ cup sweetener of choice (sugar, brown sugar, maple syrup or honey)

2 - 3 cups blueberries, or other berries/fruit of choice (strawberries/banana, raspberry, apple, or pumpkin puree are delicious)

8 large eggs

2 cups milk (whole, 2%, half & half, coconut or almond milk will work)

1 tsp. ground cinnamon

2 tsp. pure vanilla extract

2 cups of granola

Cinnamon Maple Butter,* see recipe

½ - 1 cup additions: shredded coconut, chopped nuts, baking chips (chocolate, caramel, or white chocolate) – optional

SERVES 8

SERVING SUGGESTION:
Serve warm with Cinnamon Maple Butter and whipped cream.

MORE DIFFICULT

Lightly grease 9 x 13" baking dish or line with parchment paper. Arrange half bread cubes in bottom of pan. Cut cream cheese into small cubes and layer over bread then top with half the berries. Layer with remaining bread cubes.

In a large bowl, whisk together eggs, milk, brown sugar, cinnamon, and vanilla.

Pour evenly over the pan. Press bread cubes lightly to absorb the liquid. Top with remaining berries. Sprinkle granola and other optional additions evenly on top. Cover with plastic wrap or foil. Refrigerate overnight. When ready to bake, remove from the refrigerator. Preheat oven to 350 degrees. Bake covered with foil for 30 minutes. Remove foil and bake for another 30 minutes or until golden brown. Remove from oven and cool for 5 minutes.

*Cinnamon Maple Butter is a guest favorite served every morning at Jewel Lake B & B. It's wonderful on toast, pancakes, waffles or French toast and also freezes well.

CINNAMON MAPLE BUTTER

1 cup butter, softened

¼ cup powdered sugar

½ cup maple syrup

2 tsp. ground cinnamon

1 tsp. pure vanilla extract

Place everything except vanilla in a mixing bowl and beat with an electric mixer for 3-5 minutes, until light and fluffy, add vanilla and mix thoroughly. Store in refrigerator or freeze.

ALMOND COFFEE CAKE

THE CROWN • OWNER SARA COX • BRECKENRIDGE, COLORADO

The Crown is located on beautiful Main Street in Breckenridge and is representative of a new generation of hybrid coffee shops, offering delicious coffee drinks and traditional coffee shop items plus so much more. Sara Cox, the proprietress serves a breakfast of champions: cappuccinos and coffee cake, and many more unique menu items.

3 cups flour, sifted

½ tsp. baking powder

½ tsp. baking soda

1 tsp. kosher salt

¾ cup unsalted butter

1 ½ cups + 2 Tbsp. brown sugar

5 eggs

2 cups buttermilk

½ cup whole milk

2 tsp. vanilla extract

1 Tbsp. almond extract

½ tsp. cinnamon

½ cup almonds, slivered

White Frosting, see recipe

SERVES 6

EASIEST

In a mixer with paddle attachment, cream butter and 1 ½ cups brown sugar. Next, add eggs, buttermilk, whole milk, vanilla extract and almond extract. Mix until incorporated. In another bowl, sift flour, baking powder, baking soda, and salt together. With mixer on low, add dry ingredients to wet slowly. Mix until smooth, about 45 seconds. Make crumble topping by mixing 2 Tbsp. brown sugar, cinnamon and almonds. Spray 13 x 9 x 2" pan with cooking spray, pour batter and sprinkle on crumble topping. Bake at 350 degrees for 40-45 minutes. This recipe could also work in a Bundt pan.

WHITE FROSTING

1 cup powdered sugar, sifted

1 tsp. almond extract

5 Tbsp. heavy cream

Mix all ingredients until smooth.

SERVING SUGGESTION:

Once cake is cool, drizzle with White Frosting, if desired. Serve plentiful slices.

PHINEAS DUTCH-BABY PANCAKES

PHINEAS SWANN BED & BREAKFAST • CHEF DARREN DREVIK • MONTGOMERY CENTER, VERMONT

The Dreviks, co-owners of Phineas Swann, vow to use local resources from Vermont farms to create outstanding and memorable breakfasts that carry skiers throughout their mornings on the hills of Jay Peak Resort, and well into the afternoons without having to take a break. Phineas Swann tries to always procure local ingredients: cooking with local farmers' eggs, bacon, sausage, and King Arthur flour from Norwich, Vermont.

1 ½ cups milk

1 cup flour

6 eggs

2 Tbsp. butter

2 cups apples, freshly peeled or canned

3 Tbsp. cinnamon

Powdered sugar

SERVES **4**

Preheat oven to 400 degrees.

Mix together milk, flour and eggs. In a small ramekin or other ceramic dish with sides, heat 2 Tbsp. butter until butter is melted, but not yet brown. Pour egg mixture into ramekin, filling dish ¾ full. Bake for 12 minutes.

Stew apples and mix with cinnamon. Cook until soft and warm.

Remove pancake from oven, fill with apple mixture, top with powdered sugar and serve hot.

SERVING SUGGESTION:
To achieve a Vermont ski-lodge feel, drizzle with Vermont maple syrup.

COCONUT FRENCH TOAST
with Prickly Pear Syrup

ST. REGIS DEER VALLEY • PARK CITY, UTAH

1 can coconut milk

3 eggs

Pinch cinnamon

Pinch kosher salt

2 tsp. powdered sugar

½ Tbsp. clarified butter

3 cubes brioche

3 fresh blackberries

3 fresh raspberries

¼ cup whipped cream, freshly whipped (optional, make Chantilly cream by adding vanilla flavoring)

Prickly Pear Syrup, see recipe

S E R V E S 1

 MORE DIFFICULT Whisk coconut milk, eggs, cinnamon, salt and sugar. Set aside. Heat griddle or pan to medium heat. Add butter and spread. Dip brioche cubes in batter and sear on all sides until golden brown and crispy. Arrange on a plate with cream and berries.

PRICKLY PEAR SYRUP

5 ripe prickly pear fruit, cleaned

1 cinnamon stick

1 cardamom pod

1 cup water

Tie cinnamon stick and cardamom pod in a sachet. Simmer all ingredients for 30 minutes. Remove sachet and puree fruit to a smooth consistency.

SERVING SUGGESTION:

Garnish with Prickly Pear Syrup and a dusting of powdered sugar.

DUTCH BABY PANCAKES

HOTEL JEROME • CHEF ROB ZACK • ASPEN, COLORADO

It has been said that a great chef must begin with some natural talent, add to that a superior palate, an inventive mind, and fortitude for an abundance of hard work and that innate talent can flourish. This is the definition of Chef Rob Zack's journey back to the Rocky Mountains and a return to Hotel Jerome.

2 ⅓ cups all purpose flour

⅓ cup + 1 Tbsp. sugar

½ tsp. salt

4 Tbsp. butter, melted

2 ¼ cups milk

4 eggs

4 egg whites

1 Tbsp. vanilla extract

1 vanilla bean, scraped

2 apples, peeled, cut in half and seeded

8 Tbsp. butter for 4 small cast iron pans

Lavender Sugar, for garnish, see recipe

SERVES 4

MORE DIFFICULT

Place flour, sugar and salt in a food processor and mix for 20 seconds to combine. Add melted butter and mix until crumble is the size of tiny peas. Place milk, eggs, egg whites and vanilla in the blender and process for 20 seconds then add flour mixture to blender and process until the batter is smooth. Batter can be made the evening before and stored in the refrigerator.

Preheat oven to 425 degrees. Place cast iron pans over medium-high heat and add 2 Tbsp. butter to each pan along with one apple half in each pan. Cook until apple is slightly caramelized and starts to soften. Pour 1 ½ cups batter into each pan around the apple half. Remove from stovetop and place in oven. Bake for 15 minutes, until puffed around edges and sides of pancake are golden brown. About 2 minutes prior to being done, cut a small slit in the middle of the pancake to release steam and dry interior of pancake.

LAVENDER SUGAR

2 Tbsp. dried lavender

2 cups sugar

1 vanilla bean

Combine lavender and sugar in a spice grinder. Blend until the consistency of powdered sugar. Remove and store at room temperature in a container with the vanilla bean.

SERVING SUGGESTION:
Sprinkle with Lavender Sugar.

MONKEY BREAD

HOVEY & HARRISON • EDWARDS, COLORADO

Gretchen Hovey and Molly Harrison debated whether to share this impeccably perfect recipe; the Monkey Bread is beloved by the community. Gretchen Hovey is dedicated to eating locally produced good food. She believes everything one needs to thrive is located within their immediate environment, which is why she started Ripe, a produce market and distribution company that works with small farmers sourcing the best that Colorado has to offer. Molly Harrison has a diverse culinary background. After working in and running top restaurants in Chicago, Atlanta and New York she moved to the mountains and helped develop the bread program for Zino's, Mountain Standard and Sweet Basil. Together Hovey and Harrison have created a communal space where local, whole, and seasonal ingredients are used to craft good food that harmonizes with planet and community.

2 ½ cups milk, scalded

1 ¼ lb. butter, softened

6 cups all purpose flour

½ cup sugar

2 - 3 oz. fresh yeast (if kitchen is hot use 2, if colder use 3)

1 Tbsp. + pinch salt

4 cups brown sugar

3 Tbsp. cinnamon

SERVES 4 - 6

SERVING SUGGESTION:
The Monkey Bread is fun to pull apart – relish eating with your hands!

MORE DIFFICULT

Scald milk over medium heat, as it cools add ¼ lb. butter and cool to under 100 degrees, if milk is too warm yeast will not work. With dough hook on mixer, place flour, sugar, yeast and 1 Tbsp. salt, turn on slowest speed and pour in milk mixture. Mix dough for 3 - 5 minutes until gluten starts to form. Once dough is mixed, cover with a damp towel to prevent a skin from forming and let rise until double in size, about 30 - 45 minutes.

While dough is rising, melt remaining butter, set aside. Mix together brown sugar, cinnamon and pinch of salt. Once dough has risen, flatten dough on table and cut into 1" bite size chunks. Dip chunks into butter then immediately toss in brown sugar mixture, coating fully. Scatter all dough bits into a buttered loaf pan or bundt pan. Bake at 350 degrees for 25-30 minutes or until golden brown then cool in the pan. Remove bread from pan and drizzle with Icing over the top and sides.

ICING

2 Tbsp. melted butter

2 Tbsp. milk

4 - 5 cups powdered sugar

¼ tsp. vanilla paste, thicker than extract but 1:1 substitution

Pinch salt

Whisk all ingredients together until a smooth paste forms that can be poured.

HUCKLEBERRY PANCAKES

THE RESORT AT PAWS UP • GREENOUGH, MONTANA

Drawing from the agricultural wealth of Montana and the West, the chefs at Paws Up create refined rustic ranch cuisine that articulately blends the most sophisticated culinary techniques with the freshest meats, produce and ingredients available. Huckleberries picked from the slopes of surrounding mountains complement many dishes, such as the Huckleberry Pancakes, the French toast and hand-made sausage.

4 cups flour

½ cup sugar in the raw (Turbinado is recommended)

4 Tbsp. baking powder

2 Tbsp. baking soda

1 tsp. salt

4 eggs

3 cups whole milk

¾ cup vegetable oil

1 Tbsp. vanilla paste

½ cup butter

2 cups huckleberries

2 cups granola

Huckleberry syrup, for serving

SERVES 6

 MORE DIFFICULT

In a large bowl combine flour, sugar, baking powder, baking soda, salt, eggs, milk, oil and vanilla paste, mixing well. Heat a skillet or griddle over medium heat. Add 2 Tbsp. butter; once slightly melted, add batter to the griddle to make a 4-inch pancake. Add 1 Tbsp. huckleberries and 1 Tbsp. granola to each pancake. Once browned on one side, flip and cook until lightly browned on the other side. Repeat with remaining ingredients.

SERVING SUGGESTION:
Top these delicious pancakes with huckleberry syrup.

BISCUIT FRENCH TOAST STICKS

BUTLER'S PANTRY AT BUTLER HOUSE STOWE INN • CHEF ZOE BIRON • STOWE, VERMONT

Biscuit French Toast Sticks were magically born out of necessity: how to inventively use extra biscuits. Chef Zoe and her team sliced them, and dunked them in batter and voilà! Not printed on the menu, in-the-know customers would order the "special secret menu item".

BISCUITS

4 cups all purpose flour, plus extra for shaping

2 tsp. salt

2 Tbsp. baking powder

1 tsp. baking soda

¾ cup cold butter, unsalted

2 cups buttermilk

FRENCH TOAST BATTER

6 eggs

2 cups milk

1 Tbsp. vanilla extract

1 Tbsp. cinnamon

¼ cup sugar

¾ cup all purpose flour

½ tsp. salt

SERVES 8

MORE DIFFICULT

For biscuits, preheat oven to 400 degrees and line a sheet tray with parchment paper. Mix dry ingredients in a large bowl until combined. Grate butter into flour mixture. Hand-toss butter and flour mixture until crumbly. Fold in buttermilk with a rubber spatula until dough starts to combine. Do not over work dough! Place dough on a floured surface and push all pieces into a mound. Shape into a rectangle, fold in half then shape into a square about 1 ½" thick.

Cut squares 3 x 3" to make 9 biscuits. Place biscuits on prepared tray with an inch between them. Bake for 15 - 20 minutes until golden brown. Remove from oven and cool completely.

In a large bowl, mix all French toast batter ingredients together until combined with a mixer or immersion blender. Slice cooled biscuits into 3 or 4 even strips. Dunk biscuits into batter and fry in a hot, oiled skillet. Cook sides until golden brown.

SERVING SUGGESTION:
Serve Biscuit French Toast Sticks with a dusting of powdered sugar; don't forget the Vermont maple syrup!

MAPLE APPLE CUSTARD TORTE

LIBERTY HILL FARM & INN • ROCHESTER, VERMONT

Vermont is the nation's leading producer of maple syrup. Vermont produces approximately 2 million gallons of maple syrup annually. This covers almost 50% of the United States' maple syrup needs.

Apple Mixture, see recipe

Batter, see recipe

¼ cup maple sugar crystals

1 cup almonds, sliced

Whipped cream or ice cream, for garnish

SERVES 12

SERVING SUGGESTION:
Serve with whipped cream or ice cream.

MORE DIFFICULT

Spoon Apple Mixture into greased 10-inch spring form pan. Pour Batter over Apple Mixture. Sprinkle with maple sugar crystals and sliced almonds.

Bake at 350 degrees, about 45 -50 minutes.

APPLE MIXTURE

1 egg, beaten

2 Tbsp. flour

½ cup maple syrup

1 cup sour cream

4 cups apples, peeled and sliced

Mix ingredients together.

BATTER

1 cup butter

1 cup brown sugar

1 egg

1 ½ cups flour

1 tsp. baking soda

½ tsp. salt

1 cup sour cream

1 tsp. maple syrup

Cream butter and sugar and add egg and sour cream until light and fluffy. Sift dry ingredients and add to creamed mixture along with maple syrup; beat until smooth.

NO-FAIL POPOVERS

AUTHOR JENNIE IVERSON • VAIL, COLORADO

As a home cook, Jennie aspires to have some impressive recipes in her arsenal. She would never consider herself on par with professionally trained chefs, but can fake it some of the time. She grew up enjoying popovers at sea level, yet has mastered a high elevation recipe that rises every time.

1 cup all purpose flour

2 eggs

1 cup milk

½ tsp. salt

Dash vanilla extract

SERVES **4**

EASIEST Spray popover pan or large muffin pan with non-stick cooking spray. Place pans in oven and preheat to 450 degrees. In mixing bowl, beat eggs slightly, add flour, vanilla extract, milk and salt and mix until just smooth. Remove pans and fill each halfway. Bake for 20 minutes, decrease temperature to 350 degrees and bake for 10 minutes.

SERVING SUGGESTION:
Serve hot with honey butter. These would pair perfectly with a lightly dressed green salad.

SUGARSHACK SWEET CREPE

SKINNY PANCAKE • WARREN, VERMONT

Skinny Pancake joins Sugarbush Resort in The Farmhouse with sweet and savory crepes, paninis, coffee, beer and wine. Skinny Pancake is committed to proving that "you can eat local food every day." Crepes are commonly filled with savory ingredients such as ham, cheese, asparagus, spinach, eggs, ratatouille, mushrooms, artichokes, and various meat products or sweet ingredients such as jams, melted chocolate, whipped cream, ice cream, Nutella (a chocolate and hazelnut paste), bananas, berries, and cinnamon.

3 eggs

1 ½ cups whole milk

2 Tbsp. oil or butter, melted

1 ⅔ cups flour

¼ cup sugar

1 Tbsp. vanilla

3 tsp. unsalted butter

6 tsp. maple sugar

SERVES 1

EASIEST

Mix batter by whisking the eggs, milk, melted butter or oil, flour, sugar and vanilla together. Let it rest. Create the filling by mixing 1 tsp. unsalted butter and 2 tsp. maple sugar. Spray non-stick cooking spray on 8-inch pan. Pour ¼ cup batter into pan, swirl pan side-to-side to form an even circle with the batter and cook over medium-low heat. Cook 1 - 2 minutes per side, or until lightly browned. Remove from heat and stack until ready to serve. Spread filling on flat crepe, fold in half and cut into 3 triangles.

SERVING SUGGESTION:
Garnish the sweet crepe with Vermont maple syrup, powdered sugar and whipped cream.

GRANNY SMITH STUFFED FRENCH TOAST

RED MAPLE CATERING • CHEF JASON HARRISON • VAIL, COLORADO

Few things exist that are better than a well-planned, beautiful meal. Chef Jason brings his passion for creating playful dishes with bright colors, complex flavors, and the most artistic presentations to Red Maple Catering, which he started as a passion project and has now propelled into a successful venture earning "2018 Best Catering" by the Vail Daily.

6 Granny Smith apples, wedge cut

½ cup butter, softened

6 Tbsp. calvados

6 Tbsp. bourbon

¾ cup organic apple cider

½ cup brown sugar

1 Tbsp. cinnamon

Pinch nutmeg

Pinch allspice

1 vanilla bean, seeds and shell needed

16 oz. cream cheese, cut into small cubes

3 cups heavy cream

5 egg yolks

¾ cup white sugar

1 loaf brioche bread, sliced lengthwise for 3 or more slices

S ERVES 8

Melt butter and sauté apples. Deglaze with two liquors and allow alcohol to cook off. Add cider and reduce by ⅔. Remove from heat, cool slightly and add brown sugar, cinnamon, nutmeg, allspice, vanilla seeds, and cream cheese. Mix well and cool.

Create custard by combining cream, vanilla bean shell, and white sugar in a pot. Simmer then remove from heat. Temper in egg yolks.*

Dry brioche slices for a few hours after slicing, dip brioche into custard and place in bread pan lined with sprayed parchment. Next spread thin layer apple mixture.

Continue building layers so there are 3 layers of bread and 2 layers of stuffing at minimum. Cover with food-grade plastic wrap and then foil; this method of moisture on one side and foil on the other protects the plastic wrap from melting. Place pan in water bath and cook in a 300 degree oven for 1 ½ hours.

Remove from oven and cool for 2 hours at room temperature and refrigerate overnight. In the morning, slice into 2" thick blocks and sear on both sides in a nonstick pan until lightly browned, and warmed through.

* To temper: add a very small amount of hot liquid into eggs while constantly whisking eggs. Continue slowly adding hot liquid while whisking eggs. This will gradually raise the temperature of eggs without scrambling. After a few moments it is safe to add remaining hot liquid.

SERVING SUGGESTION:
Drizzle with maple syrup and garnish with fresh berries, crème fraiche and apples.

SWEET CREPES

GOODYS MOUNTAIN CREPERIE • CHEF DEREK RHYNER • WINTER PARK, COLORADO

Goodys prides itself on cooking from scratch every day, using only whole, natural ingredients that are additive-free. People describe Goodys' food in various ways: street food, comfort food, mountain food, but the aim is always to serve great tasting food, authentic to its roots. The chefs, cooks, bakers and baristas are chosen for their passion about what they do, and it shines through in every dish.

5 eggs

3 cups all purpose flour

½ cup butter, melted

3 cups milk

½ tsp. salt

S'mores Filling, see recipe

Strawberry Shortcake Filling, see recipe

Nutella Filling, see recipe

S E R V E S   3 - 4

 EASIEST Put all ingredients except fillings in the blender and pulse for 10 seconds, if lumps remain blend again. Batter should be runny. Refrigerate batter for 1 hour. The batter will keep for 48 hours. Or, batter can be made by mixing. Mix on medium eggs, 2 cups flour, and 1 cup milk until well combined and no lumps appear. Add melted butter and mix again. Add 1 more cup milk, salt and remaining flour and mix. Finally add remaining milk and mix.

Preheat a non-stick frying pan or griddle on medium high. Lightly butter surface of pan with a brush. Butter should sizzle - if it doesn't, the pan isn't hot enough. Pour ⅓ cup batter into center of pan and swirl to spread evenly or use a crepe spinner. Cook for 30 seconds and flip with a spatula. Cook for another 10 seconds and remove. Lay out flat and uncovered. Continue until batter is used. Keep warm in oven set on low.

S'MORES FILLING

Semi-sweet chocolate chips

Mini marshmallows

Graham crackers, crumbled

Chocolate syrup

Whipped cream, for garnish

Fold warm crepe in half. Sprinkle ¼ cup each chocolate chips and marshmallows over middle section. Fold outside edges into middle, overlapping. Top crepe with graham cracker crumbles and drizzle chocolate syrup. Dust with powdered sugar and top with whipped cream.

STRAWBERRY SHORTCAKE FILLING

1 pint fresh strawberries, stems removed and halved

¼ cup granulated sugar

Powdered sugar, for garnish

Whipped cream, for garnish

In small saucepan, cook ¾ of strawberries and granulated sugar on medium, about 5 – 10 minutes. Cool. Slice remaining strawberries ⅛" thick. Fold crepe in half, ladle compote down the center, fold crepe into thirds and top with strawberries, powdered sugar and whipped cream.

NUTELLA FILLING

Nutella

Bananas or strawberries, sliced ⅛" thick

Powdered sugar, for garnish

Whipped cream, for garnish

Soften Nutella in a bowl over boiling water. Stir often, until soft and pourable. Fold crepe in half and drizzle Nutella down center of crepe, fold sides over to the middle and top with fruit. Drizzle extra Nutella over fruit, dust with powdered sugar and top with whipped cream.

SERVING SUGGESTION:
Try with S'mores, Strawberry Shortcake or Nutella Fillings.

S'MORES TACO

TAVERN ON THE SQUARE AT THE ARRABELLE • CHEF PAUL WADE & PASTRY CHEF JENN DAVIS • VAIL, COLORADO

A S'mores Taco captures the ski town essence perfectly, because mountain enthusiasts love roasting s'mores over crackling campfires. Of course, Chef Wade elevates this dish slightly for the impeccable Arrabelle Resort, because the resort offers casual comforting cuisine, but also showcases upscale Alpine inspired dining.

2 cartons premium vanilla ice cream

1 ½ cups mini marshmallows, toasted

½ cup graham cracker crumbs

1 package pre-made waffle cones

Graham Cracker Whipped Cream, see recipe

Chocolate Sauce, see recipe

SERVES 8 - 12

Soften the vanilla ice cream. Toast mini marshmallows in oven using broiler until marshmallows are golden brown, fold toasted marshmallows into 1 carton of softened ice cream, cover and chill for minimum of 4 hours. Fold graham cracker crumbs into the other carton of softened ice cream, cover and refreeze until hardened. These ice creams can be prepared 1 day ahead. Assemble waffle cone with the 2 kinds of ice cream topped with Graham Cracker Whipped Cream and Chocolate Sauce.

SERVING SUGGESTION:
To impress your friends, you may create homemade ice creams and make your own waffle cones with Pastry Chef Jenn Davis's recipes on SkiTownLife.com.

GRAHAM CRACKER WHIPPED CREAM

2 cups heavy cream

¼ cup granulated sugar

½ cup graham cracker crumbs

Mix cream and sugar together and whip until stiff peaks form. Fold in graham cracker crumbs.

CHOCOLATE SAUCE

1 cup heavy cream

2 Tbsp. light corn syrup

1 cup semi sweet chocolate chips

Boil heavy cream and corn syrup together and pour on top of chocolate chips. Let melt, then whisk together and cool.

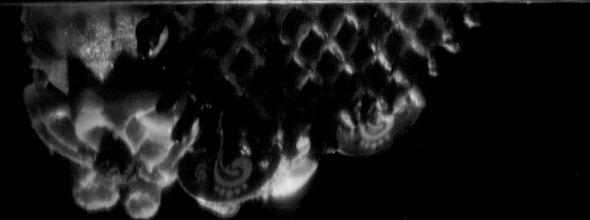

CINNAMON APPLE FRENCH TOAST
with Brie, Hazelnuts and Apricot Coulis

JUNIPER HOTEL • BANFF, ALBERTA, CANADA

There's nowhere else in Banff like the Juniper Hotel. From panoramic views, plentiful sunshine, and the natural setting to vintage modernist architecture and an intimate retreat that has been a gathering point for years. The mountains rise straight up from Juniper's back door to Banff Sunshine Village, famous for Canada's Best Snow and three mountains of diverse terrain.

6 eggs

½ Tbsp. vanilla extract

½ Tbsp. cinnamon, ground

¼ tsp. ground cloves

¼ tsp. nutmeg, freshly grated

2 Tbsp. sugar

Cinnamon Stewed Apples, see recipe

Apricot Coulis, see recipe

1 loaf soft, white bread, 1" slices

1 Tbsp. canola oil

1 Tbsp. butter

Canadian double cream brie cheese, sliced ¼" thick

SERVES 4

Combine eggs, vanilla, cinnamon, cloves, nutmeg and sugar. Preheat oven to 350 degrees. Soak 2 slices of bread in egg mixture until coated. In a large non-stick pan over medium heat, add oil and butter. Cook slices in pan until golden brown, about 3 minutes. Flip the slice, add 2 Tbsp. Cinnamon Stewed Apples to one slice and add 1 brie piece to other slice. Cook at 350 degrees for 10 minutes or until cheese is melted and bottom of slices are golden brown. Remove and close the two slices together – making a French toast sandwich. Rest for 3 minutes.

Swirl some Apricot Coulis on a plate. Slice French toast diagonally and place on a plate.

SERVING SUGGESTION:
Sprinkle French toast with powdered sugar and candied hazelnuts and drizzle with maple syrup. Garnish with lightly dressed frisée or arugula greens.

CINNAMON STEWED APPLES

1 apple, peeled and cored

1 shallot, diced

¼ - ⅓ cup brown sugar

1 Tbsp. butter

1 tsp. ground cinnamon

1 tsp. fresh lemon juice

¼ tsp. ground cloves

Nutmeg to taste

Salt and pepper to taste

Melt butter with brown sugar, cinnamon, cloves and nutmeg. Add apples and shallots, cook until apples are soft. Strain liquid and rest. Add lemon juice, salt and pepper. Pulse in a food processor until somewhat chunky.

APRICOT COULIS

1 cup apricots, dried

½ cup sugar

1 Tbsp. honey

Boil apricots to soften, drain and add apricots to blender. Puree apricots with sugar and honey until smooth. Boil mixture with 1 cup water for 10 minutes. Strain through a fine mesh. Return to heat and reduce by half.

PUMPKIN BREAD

LOG CABIN CAFÉ • SILVER GATE, MONTANA

Owner Laurie Hinck shares her exclusive Pumpkin Bread recipe from Log Cabin Café, which is located northeast of Yellowstone National Park and southwest of Red Lodge Mountain Resort.

4 Tbsp. butter

8 eggs

4 cups canned pumpkin

6 cups sugar

2 cups salad oil

7 cups flour

2 tsp. baking powder

2 tsp. cinnamon

4 tsp. baking soda

2 tsp. nutmeg

1 tsp. ground cloves

2 tsp. salt

2 tsp. allspice

1 ⅓ cup water

SERVES 10

SERVING SUGGESTION:
Delicious in every way, so serve many slices – they will be consumed!

EASIEST

Preheat oven to 350 degrees. Oil 4 large bread pans using melted butter and a brush. Beat eggs and mix in pumpkin, sugar, and salad oil. Sift flour, baking powder, cinnamon, baking soda, nutmeg, ground cloves, salt and allspice together into a large bowl. Mix wet ingredients with dry ingredients alternating with water until all are combined. Divide mixture among 4 pans and bake for 40 minutes at 350 degrees until toothpick comes out clean.

FRENCH TOAST & BERRIES

158 MAIN • CHEF JOHN (JACK) FOLEY • JEFFERSONVILLE, VERMONT

Near Smugglers' Notch Resort, a Maple Sugar Festival happens annually at Boyden Valley Winery, including infamous maple syrup sample tastings. But it doesn't stop there: maple cocktail tastings, samples of maple milkshakes made with Vermont ice maple crème, and cupcakes made with maple syrup. It's a maple syrup extravaganza!

4 large eggs

1 cup milk

¼ cup sugar

¼ tsp. salt

1 Tbsp. cinnamon

1 Tbsp. vanilla extract

1 tsp. orange peel, grated

1 Tbsp. Cointreau

3 slices baguette, diagonally sliced

SERVES 1

SERVING SUGGESTION:
Of course, serve with pure Vermont maple syrup, fresh berries and a dusting of powdered sugar.

Preheat fryer to 350 degrees. Add all ingredients, except baguette slices and whisk together. Dip baguette slices into egg mixture and fry. After 4 minutes, turn slices to cook evenly. Remove and place on kitchen towel to absorb excess oil. These can also be pan-fried with butter.

BAKED FRENCH TOAST

SNOWBERRY INN BED & BREAKFAST • CHEF ANDREA BURK • EDEN, UTAH

Powder Mountain Resort is just a hop, skip and jump from the Salt Lake City airport. This amazing 'secret spot' offers a powder day experience like no other: Snowcat Powder Safari. The all-day safari takes guests to over 3,000 skiable acres of open bowls, chutes and perfectly gladed trees.

8 Tbsp. unsalted butter, divided

⅓ cup + 1 Tbsp. brown sugar

1 ½ tsp. cinnamon

¼ tsp. nutmeg

⅛ tsp. salt

12 slices potato bread

1 ½ cups milk

4 eggs

SERVES 6

SERVING SUGGESTION:
Dust with powdered sugar and serve immediately with savory hash browns, sausage and fresh fruit.

MORE DIFFICULT

Preheat oven to 350 degrees. Combine brown sugar, cinnamon, nutmeg and salt. Mix well. Two bread slices will be used to make 3 layers in one ramekin. Using a cookie cutter cut a circle piece and half circle piece out of each bread slice. Trim crust off half circle pieces. Combine half pieces to make a complete circle. Mix milk and eggs in a mixing bowl with a pouring spout. Butter 6 ramekins with ⅛ tsp. softened unsalted butter.

Melt remaining unsalted butter in small pot. Sprinkle ½ tsp. sugar mixture into ramekin bottom. Carefully place one bread circle in ramekin bottom and brush melted butter on top of bread and sprinkle 1 tsp. sugar mixture evenly. Fit in half circle bread pieces and brush melted butter on top of bread and sprinkle 1 tsp. sugar mixture. Pour ¼ cup milk and egg mixture over the two layers of bread in the ramekin. Soak the third layer of bread in milk and egg mixture for 10 - 20 seconds; carefully place atop other layers and sprinkle with 1 tsp. sugar mixture.

Bake on sheet pan in bottom rack of oven for 30 minutes. Carefully remove French toast from ramekin with an offset spatula or butter knife.

CRAISIN WALNUT SCONE

CITY ON A HILL • CHEF MICHELLE PRENGER • LEADVILLE, COLORADO

City on a Hill is a specialty coffee roaster and coffee shop located in the Rocky Mountains of Colorado. The 'City' refers to Leadville, a historic mining community located at the base of the nation's highest peaks. Leadville is the highest incorporated city in North America.

3 ½ cups flour

⅓ cup sugar

¼ tsp. salt

¾ tsp. baking powder

¾ cup of cold butter, cut in small pieces

2 cups craisins

1 cup walnuts, chopped

2 eggs

1 ½ cups heavy cream

1 tsp. vanilla

Whole milk, for brushing

SERVES **6**

SERVING SUGGESTION:
Enjoy with a cup of La Neutral, City on a Hill's newest roast!

 EASIEST

Preheat oven to 350 degrees. In a medium-sized mixing bowl, combine flour, sugar, salt and baking powder. Cut cold butter into flour using fork or pastry blender until pea-sized then add craisins and walnuts, reserving ¼ cup for top. In a separate bowl, whisk together eggs, heavy cream and vanilla. Make a well in dry ingredients. Add liquid mixture and combine. Place dough on lightly floured surface. Pat into a 9 x 9" square, 1" thick. Cut into 6 pieces then cut each piece in half diagonally. Place on baking sheet lined with parchment paper. Brush lightly with whole milk. Sprinkle remaining walnuts on top. Bake for 20 minutes or until golden.

RYE WAFFLES

J.J. HAPGOOD GENERAL STORE AND EATERY • PERU, VERMONT

Owners Juliette and Tim Britton serve the local community at J.J. Hapgood General Store and Eatery. They strive to build a common space and everyday destination for eating, celebrating and coming together with friends and family.

1 cup all purpose flour

1 cup rye flour

2 Tbsp. sugar

1 tsp. baking soda

2 tsp. baking powder

½ tsp. salt

2 cups buttermilk

¼ cup salted butter, melted

2 farm fresh eggs

SERVES 2 - 4

 EASIEST

Sift dry ingredients together. Whisk wet ingredients in a separate bowl. Stir together until just combined. Heat waffle iron to high and butter or spray the iron. Cook using iron instructions. This batter can also be used for pancakes (pictured), but add a splash more buttermilk for a thinner consistency.

SERVING SUGGESTION:

Enjoy the waffles with J.J. Hapgood's Vermont Maple Syrup.

BEIGNETS

PIG & A JELLY JAR • HOLLADAY, UTAH

Pig & a Jelly Jar serves a fresh, from scratch menu with a unique twist on southern comfort food. What could get more southern than beignets, which are commonly served in New Orleans as breakfast items?

7 cups flour, sifted

⅛ tsp. kosher salt

1 tsp. cinnamon

¾ cup granulated sugar

2 eggs, whisked

1 tsp. vanilla

1 tsp. baking powder

2 ¼ tsp. dry yeast

1 cup warm milk

3 cups water

½ cup butter, melted

2 cups powdered sugar

Vegetable oil for frying

SERVES 6 - 8

In a bowl, combine 1 cup warm water and dry yeast. Set aside for 5 minutes. Mix all wet ingredients in a bowl. Mix all dry ingredients, except powdered sugar and 3 cups flour, in a separate bowl. With a mixer slowly incorporate dry and wet ingredients with yeast slurry. Rest for 2 minutes. Add melted butter and remaining flour until a soft and pliable consistency. Cover dough for 3 hours – the batch will rise and double.

Pull rested dough into 2" balls and flatten. Heat vegetable oil in cast iron pan to 360 degrees.

When oil is hot but not smoking add flattened dough. Make sure dough is submerged in the hot oil and rotate - do not crowd dough in pan.

Beignets will float and need to be turned in pan – process will take 3 - 4 minutes. Remove with a slotted spoon and blot excess oil using paper towels. Place hot beignets in a paper bag filled with 2 cups powdered sugar and shake.

SERVING SUGGESTION:
Beignets are best served warm and with blueberry lavender jam.

MANGO LIME CREAM
with Huckleberries

HUCKLEBERRY HILL BED AND BREAKFAST • SANDPOINT, IDAHO

At Huckleberry Hill Bed and Breakfast the daily fare is anything but ordinary, as new favorites are constantly being added to the repertoire. It is imperative to Innkeeper Gina Hurley that at least one dish highlights handpicked northern Idaho huckleberries.

2 ripe mangoes

¼ cantaloupe

2 - 3 limes, juiced and zested

¼ cup heavy cream

Huckleberries and mint, for garnish

SERVES 6

Peel and cut mangoes into cubes. Cut rind off cantaloupe and cube. Place fruits with juices and zest from limes into food processer and blend until just incorporated. Add cream and briefly blend to incorporate. This can be refrigerated for 3 hours, mix before serving. Pour into chilled serving cups.

SERVING SUGGESTION:
Top with huckleberries and garnish with fresh mint.

BAKED BLUEBERRY FRENCH TOAST

INN AT ELLIS RIVER • JACKSON, NEW HAMPSHIRE

Jackson, New Hampshire and the Inn at Ellis River are New Hampshire's best kept secrets. The Inn at Ellis River was voted "Best Bed & Breakfast" in The Conway Daily Sun's "100 Best of 2018 Mount Washington Valley" for the second year in a row.

9 large eggs

2 ¼ cups half and half

2 tsp. vanilla extract

¼ tsp. ground cinnamon

1 loaf quality white bread, cubed

1 jar blueberry preserves

4 blueberry muffins or scones, prepared

SERVES 8

EASIEST

In a bowl, whisk eggs, half and half, vanilla extract and ground cinnamon. Set aside. Cube 8 bread slices and press into glass pie plate sprayed with non-stick baking spray. Add enough egg mixture to cover bread and soak.

Spread a thin layer of blueberry preserves over bread then cube 4 more bread slices. Layer these cubes on top of preserves. Cut muffins (or scones) into pieces and layer on top with bread cubes. Cover this final layer with remaining egg mixture and soak. Cover with foil and bake at 350 degrees for 60 – 90 minutes (check after 60 minutes to determine whether "set" and cooked through).

SERVING SUGGESTION:
Serve topped with whipped cream and a side of quality maple syrup.

CINNAMON RAISIN FRENCH TOAST

THE PETTIGREW INN • LUDLOW, VERMONT

Innkeeper Courtenay Dundy has been blessed with a wanderlust allowing her to live in nine US states, the District of Columbia, and seven foreign countries; she has spent years actively cultivating her passions for travel, food, and the provision of gracious hospitality. Courtenay's love of mountains and trees led her to Vermont and The Pettigrew Inn, where she combines her passions and creates memorable hospitality experiences for friends, family, and guests.

1 loaf cinnamon raisin bread

10 eggs

1 cup heavy cream

1 cup whole milk

4 Tbsp. sugar

¼ tsp. nutmeg

¼ tsp. cinnamon

SERVES **6**

SERVING SUGGESTION:
Sprinkle with powdered sugar and serve with butter and Vermont maple syrup.

EASIEST

Remove ends from cinnamon raisin loaf and slice into 6-8 1" slabs. Lay flat in a large rectangular pan. Whisk eggs, cream, milk, sugar, nutmeg and cinnamon together in a medium bowl. Pour egg mixture evenly over top of bread slices, coating each one. Rest for 5 minutes then flip each slice so other sides rest in egg mixture. Cover pan with plastic wrap and refrigerate overnight.

In the morning, preheat oven to 350 degrees and line a baking tray with parchment paper. Preheat griddle to 350 degrees and spray with non-stick spray. Remove slices of bread from pan and cook on preheated griddle for 3 minutes, until bottoms are golden; turn and cook on other sides for 1 minute. Place slices on parchment-lined sheet pan and bake in oven for 10 minutes. Remove from oven and place on serving plate.

MORNING GLORY MUFFINS

THE WARREN STORE • WARREN, VERMONT

A 'glorious' way to start the day, Morning Glory Muffins combine the sweet taste and chewy texture of carrots with the pleasing flavors of apple, raisins, coconut, walnuts, and cinnamon.

2 cups all purpose flour

1 ¼ cups sugar

2 tsp. baking soda

2 tsp. cinnamon

½ tsp. salt

3 eggs

1 cup vegetable oil

2 tsp. vanilla

1 apple, peeled and grated

2 cups carrots, grated

½ cup raisins

½ cup shredded coconut

½ cup walnuts

SERVES 12

SERVING SUGGESTION:
These moist muffins can be simply enjoyed or enriched with a pat of butter.

Combine dry ingredients and set aside. Grate carrots and combine with raisins, coconut and walnuts. Grate apple and reserve. In a standing mixer with whisk attachment, whip eggs for one minute. Gradually drizzle in oil in a slow, steady stream then add vanilla. Squeeze any moisture from apples and add to egg mixture. Switch to paddle attachment and mix in dry ingredients. Mix in carrot mixture.

Pour muffin mixture into a greased muffin tin. Bake at 375 degrees for 25 - 30 minutes, until set and an inserted toothpick comes out clean.

COCONUT CHEESECAKE

TAVERN ON THE SQUARE AT THE ARRABELLE • CHEF PAUL WADE AND PASTRY CHEF JENN DAVIS • VAIL, COLORADO

Opulent, yet inviting, no other hotel but the Arrabelle can combine the same level of luxury and timeless elegance with the type of old-world charm that inspired so much of the Vail Valley known today. Nestled at the base of the Eagle Bahn gondola, Tavern on the Square's slope-side location is truly unbeatable, delighting taste buds with mouthwatering dishes to fuel you before or after a day on the mountain.

32 oz. cream cheese, room temperature

½ cup + 2 Tbsp. + 2 tsp. granulated sugar

1 ½ tsp. gluten free flour blend

4 eggs

¾ tsp. vanilla extract

½ cup + 1 Tbsp. sour cream

½ cup coconut milk powder

Coconut Macaroon Crust, see recipe

SERVES 6 - 8

SERVING SUGGESTION:
Serve unadorned or with fresh fruit.

In a bowl, combine granulated sugar, gluten free flour blend and coconut milk powder, set aside. In a mixer with paddle attachment, whip cream cheese until smooth, scraping sides occasionally. Add sour cream, vanilla and eggs one at a time, then add dry ingredients to wet mixture. Add mixture on top of the prepared macaroon crust in the spring form pan.

Bake at 350 degrees for 25 - 35 minutes or until center is almost set, run knife around rim of pan to loosen cake; cool before removing rim. Refrigerate for 4 hours.

COCONUT MACAROON CRUST

½ cup granulated sugar

2 Tbsp. water

2 Tbsp. light corn syrup

1 Tbsp. unsalted butter

¼ tsp. salt

½ tsp. vanilla extract

1 cup + ⅓ cup coconut, desiccated and unsweetened*

1 ½ tsp. gluten free flour blend

¼ tsp. cream of tartar

2 egg whites

Preheat oven to 350 degrees. Add sugar, water, corn syrup, butter, salt and vanilla extract in a pot. Bring to a boil and remove from heat and set aside.

Combine desiccated coconut, gluten free flour blend and cream of tartar into a mixing bowl fitted with a paddle attachment. Pour in sugar mixture from pot and mix until bottom of bowl feels cool to the touch. Slowly add egg whites until mixture is fully combined. In a well-greased 9" spring form pan, press coconut macaroon batter into bottom of pan spreading in an even layer. Bake for 10-12 minutes until lightly browned, remove from oven and set aside.

* Shredded coconut is mostly dry, but retains more moisture than desiccated coconut. But, the main difference between shredded, desiccated and flaked coconut are the shapes of the coconut. So, use shredded or flaked coconut the same way you'd use desiccated, ground coconut. It needs to be unsweetened.

CREAMY STRAWBERRY CREPES

BRASS LANTERN INN • STOWE, VERMONT

Creamy Strawberry Crepes have been a natural fit and enormous hit at the Brass Lantern Inn. They are lighter than the typical Vermont pancakes with maple syrup.

2 cups milk

4 eggs

2 Tbsp. butter, melted

1 Tbsp. sugar

1 tsp. vanilla

½ tsp. salt

1 ½ cups flour, sifted

Creamy Strawberry Filling, see recipe

MAKES 12 – 14 CREPES

MORE DIFFICULT

In a blender, mix all of the ingredients except filling until batter is very smooth, 30 - 40 seconds. Best if batter is made the evening beforehand. Melt a pat of butter on a medium-high 8 - 10" pan; butter should not burn. Pour ¼ cup batter into pan. Rotate pan to form an even thickness for the crepe. Cook 1 - 2 minutes per side or until lightly brown. Remove from heat, stack and cover with moist warm towel until ready to serve.

Spread Creamy Strawberry Filling on flat crepe and add strawberries from Creamy Strawberry Filling ingredient list. Roll the crepe into a tube.

SERVING SUGGESTION:
Sprinkle each roll with powdered sugar.

CREAMY STRAWBERRY FILLING

8 oz. package cream cheese, softened

1 ¼ cups powdered sugar, sifted

1 Tbsp. lemon juice

1 tsp. lemon zest

½ tsp. vanilla extract

1 cup heavy cream, whipped

3 – 4 cups strawberries, sliced

Blend the cream cheese, powdered sugar, lemon juice and zest, and vanilla with an electric mixer until smooth. In separate bowl, whip heavy cream until firm. Gently fold whipped cream into cream cheese mixture.

WHITE CHOCOLATE MACADAMIA NUT COCONUT COOKIES

CHILKOOT CAFÉ AND CYCLERY • BAKERS THERESA XAVIER AND MACKENZIE CLARK • STILLWATER, MINNESOTA

Chilkoot Café and Cyclery features a full service café specializing in high quality food and baked goods made from scratch. All coffee is roasted in house allowing the freshest cup to be served. Chilkoot strives to use local, sustainable and organic ingredients whenever possible.

1 cup butter, softened

¾ cup light brown sugar, packed

½ cup white sugar

2 whole eggs

1 tsp. vanilla extract

2 ½ cups all purpose flour

1 tsp. baking soda

½ tsp. sea salt

1 cup macadamia nuts, coarsely chopped

1 cup white chocolate chips

1 cup coconut, shredded

MAKES 24 COOKIES

SERVING SUGGESTION:
Make sure to place more than one cookie on an individual plate; there is no way to consume just one!

 EASIEST

Preheat oven to 350 degrees. In a large mixer bowl, cream together butter, brown sugar, and white sugar until smooth and color is light and smooth, about 2 - 3 minutes. Add eggs and vanilla. Mix until fully incorporated. Combine flour, baking soda, and salt, in a separate bowl; gradually add into the creamed mixture on low mixer speed. Mix until dough starts to come together. Add macadamia nuts, white chocolate chips and coconut to cookie dough. Then mix until fully combined. Scoop mixture with desired scoop and bake for 10 minutes in the preheated oven, or until golden brown.

SWEET POTATO MUFFINS

FIRE SIGN CAFE • TAHOE CITY, CALIFORNIA

This is a great recipe for leftover sweet potatoes that had been made for dinner the previous evening.

1 large sweet potato, cooled, peeled and diced

½ cup milk

3 eggs

¾ cup vegetable oil

2 ¼ cups sugar

1 orange, zested and finely chopped

3 ½ cups flour

2 ½ tsp. cinnamon

1 ½ Tbsp. baking powder

1 cup pecans, chopped

MAKES 24 MUFFINS

MORE DIFFICULT

Bake sweet potato the day before or use leftover sweet potatoes. After cooled, peel and dice potato. Preheat oven to 375 degrees. In a mixing bowl, combine milk, eggs, vegetable oil, 1 ¾ cups sugar, chopped oranges and orange zest and set aside. In another large mixing bowl, combine flour, 1 ½ tsp. cinnamon, baking powder and pecans.

Add wet ingredients to dry mixture and fold in 2 cups sweet potatoes. If mixture seems too dry, add a little more milk. Fill greased muffin tins just over ¾ full and sprinkle the tops of each with remaining cinnamon and sugar mixed together. Bake for 27 minutes or until an inserted toothpick comes out clean.

SERVING SUGGESTION:
Serve these muffins with a hot cappuccino.

CRANBERRY-ORANGE POWER MUFFINS

THE KINGFIELD WOODSMAN • BAKER JO SPIELVOGEL • KINGFIELD, MAINE

Baker Jo Spielvogel created this quick protein-packed, low calorie treat and Betsy Clemens, owner of The Kingfield Woodsman quickly offered it to meet the growing demand for flavorful, moist gluten-free options for breakfast on-the-go. The Kingfield Woodsman showcases 8 different flavor combinations of this particular muffin.

1 cup old-fashioned oats, puree down to powder in blender or food processor

2 scoops vanilla protein powder

2 Tbsp. fat-free, sugar-free vanilla pudding mix

1 tsp. xanthan gum

1 tsp. baking powder

1 tsp. baking soda

1 cup egg whites

½ cup non-fat, plain Greek yogurt

¾ cup sugar-free orange marmalade

1 tsp. orange extract

¾ cup frozen or fresh cranberries

SERVES 6

SERVING SUGGESTION:
Enjoy muffins grilled or heated in the microwave for about 30 seconds.

MORE DIFFICULT

Preheat conventional oven to 350 degrees or convection oven to 325 degrees. Spray large, Texas-size muffin tin with nonstick spray. In 2 separate bowls, whisk together dry ingredients then whisk together wet ingredients. Combine dry and wet. Divide batter evenly in 6 large muffin cups. Bake for 25 minutes—do not overcook. Cool in tin for 10 minutes then remove. Cool muffins on rack. Refrigerate or freeze leftover muffins.

ORANGE CUSTARD DIPPED FRENCH TOAST

THE BICKERING SISTERS • OGDEN, UTAH

The Bickering Sisters serves Real. Good. Fresh. Breakfast all day. Enjoy the Orange Custard Dipped French Toast on their menu along with other originals: 'Toad in the Hole' on an everything bagel, French toast sandwich, asparagus, feta and tomato scramble, and many other options.

8 eggs

¼ cup half and half

¼ cup pure maple syrup

1 large orange, juiced and zested

1 tsp. cinnamon

21-grain bread, sliced

2 Tbsp. butter

SERVES 8

EASIEST

Mix all ingredients together, except bread and butter. Dredge bread slices in mixture and cook on medium-high heat in a large cast iron skillet with butter. Cook both sides until crispy.

SERVING SUGGESTION:

Serve the decadent French toast slices with fresh berries, bananas and 100% pure organic maple syrup. Serve with thick sliced bacon.

CORNFLAKE-ALMOND CRUSTED FRENCH TOAST
with Maple-Walnut Butter

TRAPP FAMILY LODGE • STOWE, VERMONT

In the early 1940s, the von Trapp family toured the United States as the Trapp Family Singers, which should be familiar as "The Sound of Music" storyline, before eventually settling in Stowe, Vermont on an enchanted farm with sweeping mountain vistas reminiscent of their beloved Austria. In the summer of 1950, they began welcoming guests to a rustic, 27-room family lodge. After a fire, the Trapp Family Lodge was erected - a striking, 96-room alpine lodge situated on 2,500 acres offering magnificent resort amenities. The entire property is owned and operated by the von Trapp family and remains "a little of Austria ... a lot of Vermont"!

8 whole farm eggs

8 cups whole milk

1 tsp. cinnamon

1 tsp. nutmeg

½ cup sugar

½ orange, zested

Brioche bread, sliced ½" thick

Cornflake-Almond Crust, see recipe

1 Tbsp. butter for frying

Maple-Walnut Butter, see recipe

SERVES 6

MORE DIFFICULT

Blend eggs, milk, cinnamon, nutmeg, sugar and orange zest. Submerge and soak bread slices. Remove bread slices and dredge in Cornflake-Almond Crust mixture on both sides. In a medium skillet with butter to coat pan, cook each side for 6 - 7 minutes until golden brown. Diagonally slice French toast and place on plate and garnish with an ample amount of Maple-Walnut Butter.

CORNFLAKE-ALMOND CRUST

3 cups cornflakes

1 cup almonds, sliced

½ cup sugar

Blend all ingredients until coarse.

MAPLE-WALNUT BUTTER

1 lb. Cabot butter, room temperature

1 cup walnuts, chopped and toasted

¼ cup Trapp Maple Syrup or syrup of choice

Fold ingredients together and chill until needed.

SERVING SUGGESTION:
Serve alongside fresh fruit.

AEBLSKIVER (DANISH PANCAKES)

BRODER ØST • HOOD RIVER, OREGON

Broder Øst's menu is as unique as its name. Serving traditional Scandinavian dishes like Aeblskiver (Danish pancakes), Lefse (Norwegian potato crepes), Köttbular (Swedish Meatballs) and Uuipuuro (Finnish oven porridge).

4 egg whites

½ tsp. vanilla

1 Tbsp. sugar

1 tsp. lemon zest

½ tsp. cardamom

4 Tbsp. melted butter

2 cups all purpose flour

1 tsp. baking powder

½ tsp. salt

2 cups milk

Lingonberry jam, lemon curd and maple syrup, for garnish

SERVES **4**

SERVING SUGGESTION:
Adorn Aeblskiver with lingonberry jam, lemon curd, and pure maple syrup.

MORE DIFFICULT

Beat egg whites until stiff peaks form then mix in vanilla, lemon zest and salt. Pour in melted butter. Combine dry ingredients in a separate bowl. With a mixer on low setting, alternate small additions of dry ingredients and milk with egg white mixture until combined. Scrape sides of bowl and beat on medium speed until no lumps remain.

This recipe requires an aeblskiver pan. Cook and flip in pan, preferably with clarified butter, but vegetable oil works as well.

OATMEAL BLUEBERRY PANCAKES

SUGARBUSH RESORT • CHEF GERRY NOONEY • WAITSFIELD, VERMONT

Executive Chef Gerry Nooney leads Sugarbush's culinary efforts, whose talents can be tasted throughout the resort. A successful restaurateur prior to Sugarbush, Gerry brings a passion for food and reverence for great hospitality to Sugarbush Resort. He was classically trained in Continental Cuisine at The Hopkins Inn in New Preston, CT and also passed on his knowledge by teaching at The New England Culinary Institute. Nooney's commitment to the local food movement earned him the 'Vermont Chef of the Year' award in 2009 by the Vermont Chamber of Commerce.

1 cup oatmeal

2 Tbsp. brown sugar

1 cup milk

1 egg

1 Tbsp. vegetable oil

¼ cup flour

½ tsp. baking powder

Pinch salt

Dash fresh cinnamon

1 cup fresh blueberries

Pinch cayenne, optional

½ Tbsp. butter

SERVES 2

EASIEST

Mix oatmeal, sugar and milk together and soak overnight.

Combine flour, salt, cinnamon, baking powder and cayenne, if desired. Into oatmeal mixture, add egg and oil and blend well then add flour mixture. Mix until combined and fold in blueberries. Preheat a pan with butter and pour ½ cup batter into medium-hot pan. Cook both sides until golden. Repeat with remaining batter.

SERVING SUGGESTION:
Serve with fresh Vermont maple syrup and embellish with fresh blueberries.

APPLE CRUMBLE BRIOCHE FRENCH TOAST

SIMPLE CAFÉ • LAKE GENEVA, WISCONSIN

Simple Café hopes to 'change the world one bite at a time'. They are committed to using locally grown seasonal ingredients as much as possible, creating familiar foods with inventive twists featuring the best artisan producers of southeastern Wisconsin. Simple Café is just a short drive to one of the Midwest's premier skiing destinations: Wilmot Mountain.

2 large eggs

1 cup whole milk

4 Tbsp. all purpose flour

3 Tbsp. sugar

1 Tbsp. vanilla extract

1 tsp. kosher salt

½ tsp. cinnamon

1 ¼ oz. butter, melted

Cinnamon Apples, see recipe

Crumble Topping, see recipe

Maple Syrup Infused Cider Reduction,
see recipe

3 slices brioche bread, thickly sliced

1 Tbsp. butter for skillet

S E R V E S **2**

SERVING SUGGESTION:
Dust with powdered sugar and indulge.

MOST DIFFICULT Beat eggs until no whites remain then add milk and whisk until combined. Whisk in flour, sugar, vanilla, salt and cinnamon then whisk in melted butter. Set aside. Heat heavy skillet and add butter for skillet. Dip brioche slices in egg mixture and cook in skillet until golden brown on both sides. Rewarm Cinnamon Apples in a pan and set aside. Layer French toast slices offset on a plate and top with Cinnamon Apples and Crumble Topping. Drizzle Maple Syrup Infused Cider Reduction over French toast.

CINNAMON APPLES

2 lbs. Granny Smith, Newton Pippins, or other tart baking apple*, peeled, cored and sliced into eighths

¼ cup sugar

½ tsp. cinnamon

¼ tsp. salt

2 Tbsp. butter

2 Tbsp. heavy cream (optional)

* Use different apple varieties for varying flavors and textures.

Toss and coat apples and dry ingredients in bowl. Rest for 5 - 8 minutes. Add butter and cream to hot pan then add apples with all juice. Sauté until apples are just soft with a slight bite. Remove from heat and cool.

CRUMBLE TOPPING

1 cup all purpose flour

½ cup light brown sugar

½ cup sugar

¼ tsp. salt

½ cup butter, melted

Combine and mix dry ingredients in bowl. Drizzle melted butter into dry mixture and toss with a fork until pea-sized pieces form. Spread crumbles on parchment lined baking pan and bake at 425 degrees for 5 - 8 minutes, until golden brown, but not burnt. Cool and store.

MAPLE SYRUP INFUSED CIDER REDUCTION

½ gallon apple cider, unfiltered and cold-pressed

¾ cup 100% maple syrup

1 Tbsp. fresh lemon juice

Reduce apple cider in a heavy pot until light syrupy in texture, about 1 cup. Remove from heat and add maple syrup and lemon juice. Stir until well combined and reserve.

SIDES & SIPS

RED'S IN RAMSAY'S HASH BROWNS

RED'S IN RAMSAY • CALGARY, ALBERTA, CANADA

Present in morning dishes worldwide, hash browns can be found on nearly every brunch menu.

3 Yukon Gold potatoes, medium-sized

2 - 3 Tbsp. unsalted butter

Kosher salt and pepper

SERVES **4**

EASIEST

Cut potatoes into ¼" squares. Par boil potatoes until almost done. Melt butter in sauce pan and add potatoes. Saute on medium heat until potatoes are golden brown. Add salt and pepper to taste.

SERVING SUGGESTION:
Garnish these hash browns with some fresh herbs and perfectly pair with almost any savory egg dish.

MAPLE GRANOLA

CROWS BAKERY & OPERA HOUSE CAFE • PROCTORSVILLE, VERMONT

Crows Bakery & Opera House Cafe welcomes locals and visitors to the Okemo Valley with freshly baked breads, sweet treats, and wholesome homestyle breakfast and lunch favorites. Owners George and Robin Timko are honored that their cafe with its extensive menu serves as a popular gathering spot for locals and visitors alike.

5 cups oats

1 cup wheat flakes

1 cup sunflower seeds

½ cup almonds, slivered

½ cup pumpkin seeds

½ cup sesame seeds

¾ cup maple syrup

1 tsp. maple extract

⅔ cup vegetable oil, such as soy or sunflower

SERVES 6

Mix together oats, wheat flakes, sunflower seeds, almonds, pumpkin seeds and sesame seeds. In a separate bowl, mix maple syrup, maple extract and oil. Combine both wet and dry ingredients and spread on a baking sheet and bake at 350 degrees until lightly browned or crisp to taste, about 30 minutes. Turn mixture halfway through baking to cook evenly and add extra maple syrup.

SERVING SUGGESTION:
Simply relish the heavenly crunchy bits and pieces!

CROISSANTS

VICEROY SNOWMASS • CHEF RON VILLA • ASPEN, COLORADO

Chef Ron Villa is an award-winning pastry chef with over 28 years of experience. Originally from Guam, he's spent most of his career in Guam, Japan, and Hawaii, specializing in the classical and modern French patisserie and boulangerie. In fact, Robert Purdy, Viceroy's general manager, claims Chef Ron makes the best croissant he's ever had. Courtesy of Pastry Chef Ron Villa at Viceroy Snowmass, the Croissants recipe results are buttery, flaky and utterly delicious.

3 ½ cups bread flour

2 tsp. salt

2 ¼ tsp. instant yeast

½ cup plus ½ Tbsp. cold water

½ cup plus ½ Tbsp. milk

2 Tbsp. butter

1 cup butter for folding (at least 83% butterfat), soften at room temperature

1 egg for egg wash

SERVES 8

Combine all ingredients, except egg for egg wash and butter for folding in a mixer with dough hook attachment. Mix on low for 3 minutes. Increase speed to medium and mix for 12 minutes. Form dough into a ball and wrap loosely in plastic wrap. Refrigerate overnight.

Place butter for folding in a quart-size plastic bag. Flatten into a square with a rolling pin. Refrigerate. Once hardened, free butter from bag by cutting around plastic edges. Soften at room temperature until slightly pliable. Roll croissant dough to same height and twice length of butter. Place softened butter in center and fold edges of dough toward center. Roll out dough to 4 times the length. Fold one end of dough ¼ up towards the middle. Fold the other end of the dough ¾ up towards the other end to meet. Fold dough in half and refrigerate for at least 15 minutes.

Roll dough to 4 times its height, fold one end of the dough ⅓ up towards the center, and fold the other end of the dough to overlap the fold. Refrigerate for at least 1 hour before making croissants. Roll dough lengthwise to slightly less than ¼" thick. Cut 4 x 8" triangles. Pick up wide side of triangle and stretch dough for a longer triangle. Place flat and roll base of triangle towards tip of triangle to form croissant. Place on parchment-lined sheet pan, 4" apart. Allow to rise, covered with a cloth for 1 ½ hours until doubled in size. Lightly brush with egg wash. Bake at 350 degrees for 35 minutes. Cool on a rack.

SERVING SUGGESTION:
These delicacies are absolutely perfect as baked.

PLUMPJACK GRANOLA

PLUMPJACK AT SQUAW VALLEY INN • OLYMPIC VALLEY, CALIFORNIA

This crunchy, fruity, cinnamon-scented wake-me-up recipe also makes a great midday snack. PlumpJack Granola can be stored for up to three weeks in an airtight container.

¾ cup unsalted butter

1 cup honey

1 ½ cups maple syrup

4 cups rolled oats

½ cup coconut, shredded

½ cup pecans, chopped

½ cup almonds, slivered

¼ cup sesame seeds

¼ cup flax or millet seeds

¾ tsp. ground cinnamon

½ tsp. coarse salt

1 ½ cups mixed dried fruit (any blend of raisins, cherries, cranberries, coarsely chopped apricots, figs, or others)

Canola oil for pan

MAKES 2 ½ QUARTS

EASIEST

Preheat oven to 350 degrees. In a saucepan, combine butter, honey, and maple syrup, and slowly bring to a boil over medium heat. Reduce heat and simmer for 5 minutes, stirring frequently—do not allow to boil over. In a large bowl, combine oats, coconut, pecans, almonds, sesame and flax seeds, cinnamon and salt. Pour hot mixture over dry ingredients and combine.

Lightly oil surface of large baking pan with canola oil and wipe off any excess with a paper towel. Spread granola mixture evenly on baking pan and bake for 15 minutes, stirring occasionally to prevent sticking or large clumps from forming. Remove from oven and stir in dried fruit, mixing evenly. Return baking pan to oven and bake until golden brown, 30 minutes. Cool before sealing in an airtight container.

SERVING SUGGESTION:
Serve granola with milk and fresh fruit or simply munch on its own.

BACON, SOUR CREAM & CHIVE SCONES

PUREBREAD • WHISTLER, BRITISH COLUMBIA, CANADA

"Stop at Purebread, arguably Whistler's most famous restaurant, for warm baguettes, amazing cakes, and other baked goodness", highlights the article 'Ski Report: What to See/Do/Wear in Courchevel, Sun Valley, and Whistler' on the Goop. com website.

3 ¼ cups flour

1 Tbsp. baking powder

½ tsp. baking soda

¼ cup sugar

1 tsp. salt

Pinch pepper

12 slices bacon

1 ½ cups cheddar cheese

½ cup chives, chopped

1 cup cold butter

½ cup whipping cream

1 cup sour cream

Egg for egg wash

MAKES 16 SCONES

 EASIEST

Cook bacon by broiling or pan-frying over medium heat until lightly crispy then chop cheddar cheese into small cubes and finely chop chives. Preheat oven to 375 degrees and line a baking sheet with parchment paper. When bacon has cooled, chop into small pieces. For best results, use butter straight from refrigerator and cut into ½" cubes. Whisk together flour, baking powder, baking soda, sugar, salt, and pepper in a large bowl. Rub cold butter cubes into flour mixture with fingertips, until dime-sized pieces. Add chopped bacon, cheddar cheese and chives and mix until incorporated. In a small bowl, mix sour cream and whipping cream and add butter mixture and mix until dough forms. Place dough on a lightly-floured surface, pat down and cut as desired—handle the dough as little as possible. Place scones on prepared baking sheet, brush with egg wash and bake for 20 minutes, until golden brown and toothpick comes out clean.

SERVING SUGGESTION:

Simply enjoy or add a pat of butter to the warm scone.

ENERGY BARS

THE INN AT WEATHERSFIELD • PASTRY CHEF STEPHANIE TAFT • PERKINSVILLE, VERMONT

The Inn at Weathersfield is a Vermont boutique inn and the home of The Hidden Kitchen, a farm-to-table restaurant and cooking classroom. Such classes as 'Cooking with Herbs' and 'Wild Edibles and Foraging' have been offered, in addition to 'Let's Do Brunch' featuring chai fruit compote with yogurt parfait, crème Brule French toast with berries, scones with two special butters, savory waffles, and poached eggs with homemade tomato jam.

1 cup honey

1 cup butter

1 ⅓ cups brown sugar

12 cups oats

1 cup raisins

1 cup cranberries, dried

1 cup dates, chopped

1 cup sunflower seeds

1 Tbsp. cinnamon

MAKES 48 BARS

EASIEST

Chop dates and combine with oats, cinnamon, seeds and fruit. Hand-mix to separate fruit. Gloves are recommended. In a pot, boil honey, butter and brown sugar for two minutes. Remove from heat. Add liquid to dry ingredients and mix until combined. Scoop onto parchment-lined sheet pan and press tightly. Refrigerate for 5 minutes, then cut into portions.

SERVING SUGGESTION:
The bars will keep for 2 weeks at room temperature and longer if stored in the refrigerator.

THE INN AT
WEATHERSFIELD

IW

VERMONT
weathersfieldinn.com

BLUEBERRY MAPLE SAUSAGE

OMNI MOUNT WASHINGTON RESORT • CHEF JACKY FRANCOIS • BRETTON WOODS, NEW HAMPSHIRE

Homemade breakfast sausage is fabulous because its one of the easiest sausages to make, it tastes far better than store-bought and it doesn't require sausage casing, if you don't have the materials or inclination. The sausages can merely be shaped into patties and sautéed so that the aroma fills a morning kitchen.

1 lb. boneless ground pork

1 tsp. kosher salt

1 Tbsp. frozen blueberries

1 medium garlic clove, minced

½ tsp. ground black pepper

1 Tbsp. ice water

1 Tbsp. maple syrup

Plastic wrap

MAKES 4 PATTIES

EASIEST

Combine pork, salt, blueberries, garlic and pepper. Toss to distribute the seasonings. Add the water and maple syrup to the meat mixture and mix until uniform in appearance.

Sauté a sample of the sausage until done, taste, and adjust the seasoning if necessary.

Shape into patties and refrigerate or freeze until ready to cook. The sausage mixture can also be rolled into a log and wrapped in plastic wrap. Freeze and slice into patties.

Gently sauté or roast the sausage to an internal temperature of 150 degrees.

SERVING SUGGESTION:
Serve aside your favorite breakfast egg dish.

HEALTHY OATS

BERT'S CAFE • SOUTH LAKE TAHOE, CALIFORNIA

Bert's Cafe is a family owned and operated diner that has been an adventurer's go-to breakfast spot since 2002. For the outdoor enthusiasts, Bert's Cafe kickstarts their day with nutritious and energizing options, such as Healthy Oats. This recipe provides the perfect energy needed to last hours on any trail or ski slope. Each bowl is made to order and the sweet, hot cereal will hit the spot and get the day going for whatever adventure is on the agenda!

2 cups regular oatmeal (not instant)

¼ cup grits

¼ cup cream of wheat

¼ cup sunflower seeds (raw, not roasted or salted)

¼ cup 9-grain mix

1 cup whole milk

Raisins

Bananas

Blueberries

Brown sugar

SERVES 1 - 2

SERVING SUGGESTION:
Serve very warm with sliced bananas and blueberries.

Mix oatmeal, grits, cream of wheat, sunflower seeds and 9-grain mix and place in storage container for use. In a small pot, add milk with ½ cup dry mixture. Mix with desired amount of raisins and brown sugar. Stir regularly at a low boil. When mixture reaches desired consistency, pour into a serving bowl.

GRANOLA

CAFE GENEVIEVE • PASTRY CHEF AMY OLDIS • JACKSON, WYOMING

Cafe Genevieve is located in a historic log cabin in downtown Jackson, Wyoming, serving inspired home cooked classics. Cafe Genevieve lures guests in with its cozy, welcoming ambiance. The cafe has been named as "Fit for Foodies", "Neighborhood Gem", and "Best Service" by OpenTable diners and has received an Award of Excellence from TripAdvisor year after year.

2 cups butter, unsalted

1 vanilla bean

¾ cup oil

1 cup maple syrup

14 cups oats, old fashioned

5 cups coconut, sweetened and shredded

1 ¼ tsp. kosher salt

2 ½ cups dried cranberries

1 ½ cups dried blueberries

MAKES 6 QUARTS

SERVING SUGGESTION:
Relish this granola knowing it is one of the featured items on Cafe Genevieve's menu.

Place butter in medium pot. Cut vanilla bean lengthwise and scrape out seeds. Add pod and seeds to pot. Cook over medium heat for 15 minutes, until golden brown. Stir frequently. Cool slightly and combine with oil and maple syrup. In a bowl, combine oats, coconut and salt. Add liquid to oat mixture and incorporate. Divide between 4 sheet pans. Bake at 325 degrees, rotating and stirring frequently until golden brown. Cool and add dried fruit.

OLD FASHIONED PORRIDGE

THE BIRCH DOOR CAFÉ • BELLINGHAM, WASHINGTON

The Birch Door Café has deep roots of restaurant excellence and expertise. It all began with Casey Nagler's grandparents' restaurant in Chicago over 50 years ago. Following in their footsteps, his parents opened the Oak Table Café in Sequim in 1981. After growing up in the family restaurant realm, Casey assisted his sister and her husband with opening their restaurant and a few years later, Casey and his wife, Taria, helped his brother and his wife open their restaurant. Carrying the flag of the family's tradition of warm hospitality and delicious food, the Naglers planted their roots in Bellingham and opened The Birch Door Café.

2 ½ cups water

1 ½ cups extra thick rolled oats

2 Tbsp. cinnamon sugar

½ granny smith apple, cored, sliced, and peeled

Small handful fresh blueberries

Small handful fresh strawberries

Small handful fresh raspberries, for garnish

S E R V E S **4**

EASIEST

Boil water in a small pot or pan. Once boiling, add oats, apple and cinnamon sugar. Cook on high heat for 5 minutes. Excess water should be gone and porridge should have a thick consistency. Add blueberries and strawberries and cook for an additional minute.

SERVING SUGGESTION:

Serve in a bowl topped with fresh raspberries. Serve with heavy whipping cream, brown sugar, and whipped butter on the side—these can be added discretionarily for desired taste.

MAPLE HONEY GRANOLA

THE WARREN STORE • WARREN, VERMONT

Mention The Warren Store and watch people's faces light up. Visitors come from near and far to eat at the deli that turns local ingredients into legendary meals. Guests can happily lose themselves for hours, browsing through the unique treasures, funky toys and fashionable finds. With these wonders under one roof, it's no wonder many say they're 'Almost World Famous'.

½ cup canola oil

¼ cup honey

¼ cup maple syrup

½ tsp. cinnamon

½ tsp. salt

½ cup almonds, sliced

½ cup cashew halves

3 cups rolled oats

½ cup raisins

½ cup dried cranberries

MAKES 5 CUPS

EASIEST

Whisk together oil, honey, maple syrup, cinnamon and salt in a large bowl. Add oats and nuts and stir until well coated. Pour onto a baking sheet and bake at 300 degrees for 20 minutes, stirring halfway through. Remove from the oven, add the fruit and cool completely.

SERVING SUGGESTION:
Layer 3 Tbsp. Maple Honey Granola, yogurt and freshly sliced fruit in tiers for a delicious parfait.

HOMEMADE ROSEMARY DIJON BREAKFAST SAUSAGE

THE BREAKFAST CLUB, ETC. • CHEF VINCE DIETRICH • LAKE PLACID, NEW YORK

The Homemade Rosemary Dijon Breakfast Sausage began as a weekend special, but soon became a staple on the breakfast menu. Chef Vince's creation is an aromatic bold sausage that fills the palate with fresh rosemary, whole grain mustard and delicate pork. This homemade sausage patty is featured in the Sausage Biscuit Benedict where the bold flavors are softened by a buttery cheddar biscuit, soft poached eggs and rich lemony hollandaise. It's also the star of the Sausage Biscuit Sandwich to which melted caramelized onion and cheddar cheese are added to the mix for an extra layer of flavor with a homemade biscuit and over easy eggs.

2 lbs. ground pork, freshly ground (unseasoned Jimmy Dean will also work)

1 Tbsp. fresh rosemary, finely chopped

¼ cup whole grain mustard (Maille Dijon Old Style is recommended)

⅓ cup unseasoned breadcrumbs

⅓ tsp. black pepper, freshly cracked

MAKES 8 PATTIES

 EASIEST

Preheat oven to 375 degrees. Combine pork, breadcrumbs, rosemary, mustard, and pepper in a medium mixing bowl. Create 8 balls then flatten into patties. Bake on baking tray lined with parchment until internal temperature reaches 160 degrees, about 18 minutes. Remove finished sausage from baking tray and drain on paper towels.

SERVING SUGGESTION:

This pairs well with any brunch cocktail but the Grapefruit Gin Gin cocktail is recommended (recipe included in Ski Town Brunch).

PURPLE YETI SMOOTHIE
with Coconut Whip

GREEN ELEPHANT JUICERY • CHEF OSHA STEARNS • VAIL, COLORADO

At the Green Elephant Juicery, the mission is simple: Make it easy for people to eat healthy foods. Smoothies are an incredible way to achieve daily requirements of protein, vitamins, minerals, and healthy fats. This juicery offers a plethora of 20+ organic smoothies, each showcasing different health benefits.

1 cup coconut milk beverage* or coconut water

1 banana

1 cup blueberries, frozen

1 Medjool date, pitted

1 Tbsp. almond butter

½ tsp. blue spirulina

½ cup ice

1 Tbsp. coconut flakes

Coconut Whip, see recipe

*Not all coconut milks are created equal: look for a good, thick coconut milk giving ¾ - 1 cup cream after refrigeration.

SERVES 1

To a blender, add all ingredients, except coconut flakes and Coconut Whip, and blend on high until smooth. Add coconut flakes and pulse 1 - 2 times until flakes are incorporated into the smoothie. Pour smoothie into a glass and top with Coconut Whip.

COCONUT WHIP

14 oz. can coconut milk, unsweetened

2 Tbsp. powdered sugar

½ tsp. vanilla extract

Refrigerate can of coconut milk overnight (at least 8 hours). Carefully open the can and separate the solid cream from the liquid. Add the cream, powdered sugar and vanilla extract to a bowl. With an electric mixer, beat on high until well mixed and peaks form, about 3 minutes. Refrigerate up to 4 days.

SERVING SUGGESTION:
Serve with a wide-opening straw or spoon.

THE BREAKFAST MARTINI

BARDENAY • BOISE, IDAHO

2 oz. Bardenay vodka (or another high quality vodka)

2 Tbsp. Orange Marmalade

SERVES 1

EASIEST

Shake with ice and strain into a martini glass.

SERVING SUGGESTION:
Garnish with an orange peel.

BRECKENRIDGE COFFEE

THE CROWN • BRECKENRIDGE, COLORADO

½ oz. Baileys or Irish cream

½ oz. hazelnut liquor

½ oz. Kahlúa or coffee liquor

Hot brewed coffee

SERVES 1

EASIEST

Combine all liquors mixing until incorporated. Add liquor mixture to a mug of hot coffee.

SERVING SUGGESTION:
Top with whipped cream.

GRAPEFRUIT GIN GIN

THE BREAKFAST CLUB, ETC. • HEATHER LEPERE • LAKE PLACID, NEW YORK

While handcrafted Bloody Marys and Mimosas get the most attention at The Breakfast Club, Etc., the Grapefruit Gin Gin is an unexpected change of pace. Take advantage of fresh squeezed grapefruit juice and a local gin (The Breakfast Club, Etc. uses Blue Line Gin) to fashion a delightfully different brunch cocktail.

1 ½ oz. gin

½ oz. peach schnapps

2 oz. fresh squeezed grapefruit juice
(pink grapefruit juice is recommended)

Ginger ale

Candied ginger, for garnish

SERVES 1

Add ice to a 16 oz. mixing glass. Add gin, peach schnapps, and grapefruit juice and shake well. Transfer the drink and ice into a fresh 16 oz. glass. Top with ginger ale.

SERVING SUGGESTION:
Garnish with candied ginger.

BLUEBERRY & BABY KALE SMOOTHIE

WHITEFACE LODGE • LAKE PLACID, NEW YORK

Evoking the region's 19th-century heyday with a wood-beamed exterior, cozy carpet-strewn sitting rooms and cast-iron fireplaces, Whiteface Lodge is nestled in Adirondack Park. This six-million-acre recreation area in upstate New York has drawn nature lovers for decades.

2 Tbsp. fresh ginger, chopped

4 large mint leaves

½ pint blueberries, rinsed and cleaned

½ cup baby kale, stems removed and rinsed

½ cup fresh orange juice

1 Tbsp. maple syrup

1 ¼ cups Greek yogurt

SERVES **2**

In a blender add ginger, mint, blueberries, baby kale, orange juice and maple syrup. Blend until ingredients are finely puréed. Add yogurt and blend on low speed until incorporated. Pour into a glass.

SERVING SUGGESTION:
Garnish with mint leaf, baby kale leaf and blueberries.

BASIL GINGER SPRITZ

RUPERT'S AT HOTEL MCCALL • MIXOLOGIST SAMANTHA SAIS • MCCALL, IDAHO

Samantha is Rupert's resident mixologist. Her flair for experimenting with classic and unique flavors results in thoughtfully created cocktails. Samantha is also a freelance photojournalist; she has traveled around the country, East Africa, parts of Europe and Central America and continues to shoot for The New York Times, Reuters, Chicago Tribune *and* The Washington Post.

1 ½ oz. gin

½ oz. basil simple syrup

2 oz. ginger beer (Fever Tree is recommended)

Splash Prosecco

1 basil leaf, for garnish

SERVES 1

SERVING SUGGESTION:
Garnish with basil leaf.

In a Collins glass, add gin, simple syrup and ginger beer. Add ice and stir. Top with Prosecco.

TAMARACK BLOODY MARY

TAMARACK BREWING COMPANY • LAKESIDE, MONTANA

The Bloody Mary mix will keep in the refrigerator for one month, so add the mix to a jar for the ability to make a delicious Bloody Mary at a moment's notice.

1 cup Worcestershire sauce

1 Tbsp. fresh lemon juice

1 Tbsp. pickle juice

1 tsp. Frank's Red Hot sauce

1 tsp. A1 steak sauce

1 tsp. horseradish

1 tsp. celery salt

½ tsp. onion powder

½ tsp. granulated garlic

½ tsp. salt

½ tsp. pepper

Premium vodka

Tomato juice

Celery, olives, and pickled vegetables, for garnish

Yields mix for **12** cocktails

Place all ingredients, except vodka and tomato juice, in a 2-cup mason jar. Secure lid and shake well. This mix will keep in the refrigerator for up to one month.

To create a Tamarack Bloody Mary, fill a pint glass with ice, add 1 ½ oz. mix and 1 ½ oz. premium vodka, and fill with tomato juice. Stir well or pour into a shaker to combine.

SERVING SUGGESTION:
Garnish with celery, olives and pickled vegetables.

VAIL MOUNTAIN

WALK OF SHAME

VINTAGE • VAIL, COLORADO

2 Tbsp. strawberry puree

1 oz. lemon vodka

½ oz. lemon juice

Sparkling wine

Lemon wheel and strawberry wedge,
for garnish

SERVES 1

In a pint glass with ice, mix together first 3 ingredients. Strain into a glass with fresh ice. Top with sparkling wine.

SERVING SUGGESTION:
Garnish with a lemon wheel and strawberry wedge.

Photography Credits

Pastry Chef Jenn Davis

Janie Osborne

Alex Mager

Dominique Taylor

Elizabeth Campbell

Danielle Visco at Luv Lens

Dave Dietrich

Laurie Z Divine Photography

McKenzie Taplin

Toni Osmundson

Sage and Scarlet Photography

Trevon Baker Photography

Shelby Bettinger

C2 Photography Chris Council and Emily Chaplin

Pastry Chef Amy Oldis

Jackie Cooper, Jackie Cooper Photo

Professional Acknowledgements

I am joyous beyond belief that Jen Baker, of Crested Butte, Colorado and Baker Standard Thyme, and I have joined culinary forces. I'm excited to gather, feast and adventure with her. Jen not only helped in restaurant selections but also copy-edited the entire manuscript for Ski Town Brunch. If more of our collaboration is of interest, venture to skitownlife.com. I am also utterly appreciative for the innkeepers, restaurant owners, chefs, sous chefs, mixologists, general managers, PR mavens and other helpful resources that assisted in making this cookbook amazingly beautiful and unique. With each new creation in the Ski Town Cookbook Collection, I gain further respect for these individuals and experts of their industries. With all the balls in the air, I am beyond thankful that Ski Town Brunch, like the cookbooks that preceded it, carved out a section on their ever-growing to-do lists. I am grateful for the creative brilliance of the photographers and designers who contributed their stunning works to this project. Additionally, Bruce Pettit continues to be a wealth of knowledge on the printing side and has managed to turn my conceptual brainchild into a tangible asset with confidence.

Last but most certainly not least, I thank my stoic sidekick—Jay Monroe of James Monroe Design, as we have been designing together for over 7 years. I genuflect to him and his ingenuity; he has been the creative calm to my many-ideas storm. With Jay's assistance, my foggy vision of this cookbook has a true clarity reflected in a beautifully and appealing design. Feast your eyes on his mastery!

Personal Dedications

Jen Baker is a true friend and confidant. I am so appreciative of her friendship and encouragement. With her by my side, Ski Town Life is more enjoyable and fulfilling each day.

My friends have constant excitement about the Ski Town Cookbook Collection. Their friendships are heartwarming and keep me motivated. It is wonderful to have figurative cheerleaders who love without conditions. My friends are additionally encouraging as they continually offer to be taste-testers and samplers of recipes. Here's toasting to you, Melissa Provencher, Sarah Johnson, Leslie do Pico, and Francesca Levaggi.

My family is my biggest motivator. I strive each and every day to love, provide and succeed for them and us. Their presence is my gentle challenge, as I believe it to be extremely important for children to see their parents succeed—I hope I am doing that in front of their eyes. Moment to moment, my three sons surprise me with their thoughtfulness: "thank you for dinner", "how is the book coming", "is there anything I can help you with" and not a tuck-in to be had without an "I love you". For them, my "sunset heart hands" may turn into "sunrise heart hands" to honor the brunch time of day.

Ross, my husband, deserves the most special dedication. Merely in his presence, I reap the benefits of his confidence and success that are constantly on an upward trajectory. He is indestructible, the most stalwart person that I know. Sunrise to sunset, he portrays qualities that I respect and strive to emulate. While he dreams grander and big picture, I dream nuances and intricacies. Together we make the whole picture; we've covered the breadth of life! Ski Town Life with Ross is ever-changing, always keeping me on my toes and boosting me out of the kitchen. We'll give those Fitbits a run for their money!

Family and friends, remember that if you eat glitter for breakfast, then you shine all day!

RESTAURANT INDEX

About the Author

Jennie Iverson is the author of *Ski Town Brunch*. She lives in Vail, Colorado with her family and is the best-selling author of *Ski Town Soups* and *Ski Town Après Ski*. Jennie is also a wife and a mother of 3 fast-growing boys with healthy, enormous appetites. Breakfast time has turned into sleeping late and lingering over brunch time or even second breakfasts during the morning, which she encourages because they can embrace the day, fully energized and then make their stamp on the world!

Jennie considers herself a gourmet in the kitchen, but more evidently a gourmand—enjoying restaurants, bistros and any dining establishment where she can sit down to others' creations. She also thoroughly enjoys traveling to other ski towns, as she relishes locals who take advantage of the out-of-doors and surrounding mountains. To sample some of the best soups for *Ski Town Soups*, appetizers and drinks for *Ski Town Après Ski*, and brunch creations for *Ski Town Brunch*, Jennie has traveled to Sun Valley, Jackson Hole, Mt Bachelor, Mt. Hood, Whitefish Mountain, Big Sky, Moonlight Basin, Heavenly, Northstar, Park City, Vail, Beaver Creek, Breckenridge, Copper Mountain, Aspen Highlands, Aspen Mountain, Snowmass, Buttermilk, Bretton Woods, Canyons, Deer Valley, Keystone, Killington, Mad River Glen, Sugarbush, Okemo, Smugglers' Notch, Steamboat, Stowe, Stratton and Whiteface. What has grown from these travel experiences and the "will travel for food" philosophy has been a perfectly balanced recipe for life: a ski town, a comfortable restaurant and a yummy food dish to share with family and friends. Reaffirming that brunch, soups for lunch and après all day are always good ideas.

Professionally and following the launch of these cookbooks, Jennie has relished in many extraordinary culinary opportunities: guest judging the Lake Tahoe soup-cooking competition, launching the inaugural Park City Soup Crawl, guest appearances at The Cottage at Mirror Lake and Omni Mount Washington Resort, covering the Stowe Wine & Food Classic, authoring monthly articles for the *Vail Daily*, blogging about Aspen's SoupSkol competition and following many renowned food events, such as Feast!Vail, Beaver Creek Food & Wine Festival, Taste of Vail, Cochon555, Denver Burger Battle, 5280 Brunch Event, Blues, Brews and BBQ and Gourmet on Gore.

Jennie Iverson has quickly become a foremost expert on ski town cuisine.